MURDER & MAYHEM
— ON —
STATEN ISLAND

PATRICIA M. SALMON

Charleston H London

THE
History
PRESS

Published by The History Press
Charleston, SC 29403
www.historypress.net

Cover images courtesy of the Library of Congress.

First published 2013

Manufactured in the United States

ISBN 978.1.62619.283.6

Library of Congress CIP data applied for.

For Barb, with Barb…

CONTENTS

ACKNOWLEDGEMENTS

Sincere thanks are extended to Barbara Hemedinger, Cheryl Criaris-Bontales, Guy Cheli, Tina Kaasmann-Dunn, Beth Gorr, Linda Cutler Hauck, Thomas McCarthy, *The Saratogian*, Dr. Shari Schindel, sioutloud, Jan Somma and the Tottenville Historical Society.

INTRODUCTION

Murders and murderers fascinate and delight us. We are drawn to the grisly details, and we follow their investigations with keen eyes and avid interest. Think of the O.J. Simpson trial. The public was never so drawn to a court case involving murder as they were drawn to that spectacle.

Some murders are neatly solved. The murdered are discovered. The murderer confesses. The murderer pleads guilty. The murderer goes to prison. Most cases are not that simple. Of course, many are never unraveled. This book presents murders that range from the clearly obvious to the completely complex. Several remain unsolved, but that might change since they are being brought to the public's attention once again.

Staten Island was originally inhabited by the Lenape, a branch of the Algonquin nation. No doubt the first murders took place on the island during the isolated years of Native American inhabitation. We have no record of their occurrences now, but we do know the arrival of white men brought Staten Island's first documented murder. It took place when Captain Henry Hudson and crew sailed into what would become the New York Harbor during September 1609. Their first meeting was positive, with green tobacco, knives and beads exchanged. Relations soured when John Colman and four crewmen left the *Half Moon* to take water depths. For an unknown reason, the party was attacked, and Colman was killed by an arrow through the throat.

After permanent settlement, various killings and murders took place on Staten Island. One early episode occurred on October 27, 1815. Bornt Lake was walking in front of his Amboy Road property in New Dorp when he was shot dead. It was no mystery who killed him, since Christian Smith ran to a neighbor pleading for advice on whether he should admit guilt or flee. The neighbor's response is unknown, but Smith was found wandering aimlessly in a local woodland that same day. Arrested, he begged for forgiveness, stating that he was justified in the act, as he had repeatedly told Lake not to trespass on his land. It seems the two had been bandying back and forth about this issue for quite some time and had made a habit of aggravating and annoying each other on every possible occasion. Neither of the two was sensible enough to stay off the other's property, so the matter escalated, ending with grievous results.

The case went before Judge Spencer, who advised the jury that Smith had no reason to kill Lake for trespassing. Smith should simply have reported the trespasser to authorities and used the law to settle the matter. But the jury disagreed, and it set Christian Smith free. The judge was astonished and told Smith, "You have another tribunal before which you must appear hereafter to answer for your crime, and where you will not have the benefit of a Staten Island jury."[1] The jury stated that its decision was based on economics. With the astronomical cost of housing, feeding and clothing a prisoner and then building a gallows for hanging, well, it was much more cost-effective to simply free the killer.

Chapter 1
THE BODY IN THE BARREL

Gentlemen of the jury, we design to show to this Court and to yourselves that that man, Edward Reinhardt, who sits before you is a bigamist with a pure girl and the murderer of the one to whom he was lawfully married and whose body we will show was the one buried in such a horrible manner by the lonely lake up on the hills of this island.
—*Prosecution statement at the murder trial of Edward Reinhardt, May 1879*[2]

There was no doubt that Edward Reinhardt had cruelly buried his wife, Annie, in a barrel at Silver Lake. She might even have been alive at the time. He admitted burying her, but ambiguity had swirled around the case ever since the body was discovered by three boys tending cattle on Sunday, September 15, 1878. The road to convicting Edward Reinhardt would be winding at best and mysterious at most.

When the body was found, Louis Reige immediately assumed it was Ellen Murphy, a woman he was unlawfully intimate with and who had gone missing. Reige headed right to the authorities with this information and was at once brought to the Richmond County Poor House at Sea View to identify the decomposing remains. As he viewed the pitiful body on the grass of the Potter's Field Cemetery, Reige burst into tears, threw himself beside it and wept convulsively. The woman was so decomposed that only her teeth and hair were recognizable. Physicians believed malpractice (abortion) had been committed, which at this time was unmentionable in polite discussion. As a result, the woman was thought to have died from internal hemorrhaging.

Reige insisted that he loved Ellen Murphy and had promised marriage once he found suitable employment. He firmly believed she was the deceased woman. The teeth matched. All who knew Ellen were aware that she did not have an unsound tooth in her head—just like the corpse on view. There was one problem though: the hair color did not correspond. Ellen's was light brown, while the deceased had dark brown hair. This mattered little at the time since Dr. William Walser stated that clothes found around the body were saturated with chloride of lime, also known as chloroform. Its presence would turn hair darker. Horrifically, the chemical-laden cloth was believed to have been placed with the body to keep the victim unconscious in case she was not dead and woke up inside the barrel. Another mixture, quick lime, had been lathered on the face to burn away the victim's features and render her unrecognizable. Not only was there an adult female body in the barrel, but there was also a self-aborted fetus. Walser acknowledged that the deceased might have died in childbirth.

Those who knew Ellen Murphy were divided. Some thought she was at a local hospital or that she had perhaps returned to Ireland in order to hide until she gave birth. Others claimed that the last time they saw Ellen, she was making her way to Manhattan for an abortion. According to Reige, she had discussed this alternative one month after discovering her pregnancy, but a doctor informed her that she needed to be four or five months along before the procedure could be performed. Rumor had it that a female abortionist, living not three hundred yards from the site where the body was recovered, was involved. Thus, she became an immediate suspect. But the case took a different turn when Gustave Keymer, rumored to be a very eccentric elderly man, came forward. While gathering watercress at Silver Lake about six weeks prior to the body's discovery, Keymer encountered a man digging a hole at the lake. When asked why he was digging, the man replied that he was burying a New Foundland dog owned by the Cisco family. It was in the barrel on the wheelbarrow he had brought with him. Keymer informed the man that if he buried the dog there, the stench would be a nuisance. As such, the man moved farther down into the ravine and recommended his labor. This was the exact location where the body was found.

On September 20, 1878, George Hommell of Saugerties, New York, accompanied by a Reverend Mr. Lichtenberg, came to Staten Island to view the body. Hommell believed the remains might be those of his missing daughter Annie. The body was exhumed. Even though the features were practically obliterated, he declared it to be his daughter, as he believed

Left: Silver Lake as it appears today. In 1878, Edward Reinhardt buried his murdered wife on the shoreline. *Photograph by Patricia M. Salmon, 2013.*

Below: Silver Lake was originally a popular resort for vacationers in the nineteenth century. *From* An Illustrated Sketchbook of Staten Island, *1886.*

the teeth and hair corresponded to Annie's. They returned to Saugerties to secure Annie's betrayer. The accused was Moses Schoenfeldt, a wealthy, married man whom Annie worked for. According to her father, appearances indicated that Schoenfeldt was on familiar terms with his daughter. Said to be pregnant, she disappeared during December 1877. Several anonymous letters received by the family stated that Annie was in New York City. In August, a letter arrived announcing that she was dead. The people of Saugerties believed that Schoenfeldt was responsible.

Moses Schoenfeldt and his wife arrived in Staten Island on September 21. Accompanied by their lawyer, the three promptly made their way to the Potter's Field Cemetery to analyze the dead woman's hair sample. Schoenfeldt emphatically stated that it did not belong to Annie Hommell. In fact, the deceased had hair that was almost two and a half feet long! After meeting with Coroner Dempsey, the couple departed, with Schoenfeldt greatly troubled about his predicament. His wife was broken down. Further complicating identification was the arrival of numerous anonymous letters declaring the woman to be someone other than Annie Hommell or Ellen Murphy. In addition, correspondence arrived claiming that Ellen Murphy was alive and well. The mystery plagued Staten Island police.

On September 26, attorney Peter Cantine and Dr. Erasmus Chipman arrived at the Poor House to have the body exhumed. Hired by George Hommell, they wanted to ascertain whether the right arm of the cadaver had ever been fractured, as Annie's had been at the age of seven. According to one local paper of the time:

> *Three able-bodied paupers were set to work to open the newly made grave in the wretched cemetery on the hillside, and in about half an hour, a rude deal box was brought to the surface. It was roughly hauled from the deep pit in which it had been deposited, the lid was loosened with a hatchet, and the offensive contents were once again disclosed to view. Simultaneously with the opening of the box, a horrible smell of putrefying flesh pervaded the little wooded graveyard. The first thing done by the Doctors was to cut off both arms close to the shoulder-blade and to boil them in an out-building attached to the Poor-house, for the purpose of facilitating the work of removing the flesh from the bones. An insane pauper, who was detailed by Overseer McCormack to superintend the boiling of the arms, completed the preliminary at nightfall and served them up to the doctors with a grin of ghastly satisfaction. A critical examination failed to disclose the remotest sign of a fracture or dislocation… the anatomy of both arms were perfect.*[3]

The woman was not Annie Hommell.

Still, there was no sign of Ellen Murphy. By early October, no fewer than thirty missing women would be reported after the public heard of the body in the barrel at Silver Lake.

On October 3, 1878, Coroner Dempsey, accompanied by Gustave Keymer, went to Manhattan to locate the mysterious barrel burier. On a previous search, Keymer had pointed a suspect out, but police declined to

The unidentified remains of Annie Reinhardt were originally placed at the Richmond County Poor House Potter's Field. *From* A Memorial History of Staten Island, *1898.*

arrest him. The same man was found once more. His name was Edward Reinhardt, and he acknowledged living on Staten Island until the previous July. While living on the island, he ran a candy store on Gore Street (now Broad Street) in Stapleton. Reinhardt emphatically denied burying a barrel at Silver Lake or ever meeting Keymer. Furthermore, Reinhardt said that he had married Pauline Dittmar seven months earlier. Reinhardt was informed by Dempsey that he must appear at the next jury sitting relative to the dead woman found in the barrel at Silver Lake on Staten Island.

Coroner Dempsey was soon visited by Charles Herborn, publisher of the German-language newspaper *Der Deutsche Zeitung*, on October 6. Under oath, Herborn stated that Edward Reinhardt was a tenant in his house and that he had a wife in the family way. Owing to Reinhardt's actions, Herborn believed he did away with her. With that, Reinhardt was arrested. In front of the judge, Reinhardt insisted that he was unmarried while living on Staten Island and that he had married Pauline Dittmar after moving to Manhattan on July 13. While on Staten Island, he claimed to live with a girl named Mary Ann Keegan, whom he stated was very much alive and living in Manhattan. Furthermore, he would produce her at any given time in order to prove that she was not the woman in the barrel. He confirmed that Keegan was expecting while he lived with her. Stating that he often pushed wheelbarrows, he argued that only once had he pushed a barrow to Silver Lake and that it was only to pick up a load of wood. Reinhardt claimed that Mary Ann Keegan left him on the morning of July 20 because he refused to marry her.

Mrs. Herborn swore on the stand that Reinhardt moved in on about April 15, 1878, and that the woman who came to live with him shortly thereafter called Reinhardt her husband. The woman told Mrs. Herborn that Reinhardt treated her badly and that she feared him. Mrs. Herborn described the wife as being low-spirited and weepy. Eventually, the wife became so distraught that she pleaded with Mrs. Herborn to help her. Mrs. Herborn declared that she "often heard the woman upbraid Reinhardt for ruining her," with him responding that "he was tired of her; that she was a burden to him."[4] Mrs. Herborn never saw the woman after the evening of July 19, but the following morning, she heard Reinhardt in the yard yelling up to the window for Annie to get up in order to visit her mother. Mrs. Herborn never heard a reply. Shortly thereafter, Reinhardt announced to Mrs. Herborn that the woman had left for her mother's. As he prepared to move from the premises, Reinhardt told Mrs. Herborn that he had a barrel of crockery to deliver to his sister's house. The barrel was covered by a piece of carpet, under which was coarse sacking that turned out to be a malt bag marked with the company name of Nuedlinger and Schmidtt. The only Staten Island brewery to use malt from this firm was the Rubsam and Horrmann Atlantic Brewery. It was located no more than a half mile from the Herborn property. The barrel, carpet and sacking were wound twice around by a cord. It was a heavy delivery to move—so heavy, in fact, that the wheelbarrow broke under its weight and Reinhardt had to borrow another. He did, and he was soon observed heading up the Richmond Road (now Van Duzer Street). According to Mrs. Herborn, after the errand, Reinhardt returned relaxed and joyful. Mr. Herborn recalled that he heard sawing on the evening of July 19 and that on the following morning, he found a sawn-off section of barrel in the yard of his house. The barrel Reinhardt pushed would soon be traced to the Bechtel Brewery, which was visible from the windows of Herborn's house.

Police searched for Mary Ann Keegan at the Manhattan addresses provided by Reinhardt. No such person was found. When questioned by reporters, Reinhardt's sister, Mrs. Lawrence Ketner, said she knew no Mary Ann Keegan. The only woman she knew who lived with Reinhardt was

The beer barrel that held Annie Reinhardt's dead body came from the George Bechtel Brewery in Stapleton. *From* An Illustrated Sketchbook of Staten Island, *1886.*

Annie Degnan. Most importantly, Reinhardt had not delivered a barrel of crockery to her residence on July 20, 1878. Mrs. Ketner also stated that in late August, she thought to visit her brother at his Broome Street, Manhattan residence. When she arrived, a woman answered the door who claimed to be Reinhardt's wife, to which Mrs. Ketner replied, "No, you are not," as Mrs. Ketner knew her brother's wife to be Annie Degnan.

Sometime before October 8, Staten Island police discovered that an Annie Degnan was reported missing by her Newark, New Jersey family. Police soon realized that the description of the body discovered at Silver Lake bore a striking resemblance to Annie. Indeed, it was also reported that Degnan was the wife of Edward Reinhardt. They had been married at Saint Paul's Episcopal Church in Newark on November 24, 1877. Police also unearthed the fact that Reinhardt had spent a year and a half in the New Jersey State Prison for stealing $2,000 worth of furs from his former employer, Coney & Stewart. After release, he worked at a celluloid factory. It wasn't long before he was back to his old habits and was again imprisoned for stealing.

Around the third week of September 1878, Edward Reinhardt visited Annie Degnan's mother to borrow money, something he did quite often. He told Mrs. Degnan that Annie was expecting a child and that they needed some cash to help them along. When asked by Mrs. Degnan how Annie was, Reinhardt replied, "Tip top."

For her part, the second Mrs. Reinhardt, Pauline Dittmar, explained to authorities that she and Reinhardt had been married on July 13. On July 20, furniture was delivered to and housekeeping began at Broome Street. In addition, Reinhardt brought two shawls and a unique ring of gold with two hearts held in chased fretwork for his bride. Annie's mother and younger brother examined Reinhardt's gifts and had no trouble identifying the items as having belonged to Annie Degnan. Owing to his proliferation of wives, Edward Reinhardt was now being referred to as the "Dandy Dutchman." No matter, Pauline Dittmar proclaimed that she would stand by her husband until he confessed to the murder of Annie Degnan, something she knew would never happen since he was "too kind" to do such a thing. Hearing that he was subjected to awful prison fare, she announced her departure for Staten Island to cook and bring him his meals. It was her belief that Annie Degnan was alive and remaining concealed to cause great trouble for Edward Reinhardt. Her husband agreed, stating that Degnan only wanted to annoy him. At this point, all concurred on one thing: even if Reinhardt refused to admit it, he was, in the least, a bigamist.

At the coroner's inquest on October 9, 1878, Rosanna Degnan positively identified the sample of hair removed from the Silver Lake barrel body as belonging to her daughter Annie. When the prisoner was brought before her, she shouted, "You vagabond, you have murdered my child!" As an overflow crowd viewed the proceedings, Annie's aunt, Ellen Fallon, testified that the shawl found on the deceased had been made by her own hand. She identified the unusual stitch that she herself had designed. Fallon concurred that the length of hair presented came from the head of Annie Degnan, proclaiming that Annie had a splendid head of hair almost two feet long that she would twist and roll around her head. Ellen Fallon also reported that Annie told her of Reinhardt's response to her delicate condition—to get rid of the consequences. Annie told her aunt she was sorry to have married Reinhardt.

Under oath, Pauline Dittmar soon testified that shortly after the Degnan inquest began, Reinhardt left with a section of loose Brussels carpet that had been in their apartment. He carried it in a basket. When asked if he had been gone long enough to throw it in the river, she responded in the affirmative, and she replied "yes" when asked if he returned with an empty basket. It turned out that the carpet was very similar to what had covered the barrel on the wheelbarrow.

Mrs. Herborn recounted how she found Annie with a bloodied mouth and chemise the week before Reinhardt moved. Annie acknowledged it was Reinhardt's doing.

Held in the Richmond County Jail, Reinhardt kept busy—so busy, in fact, that one of his jail keepers discovered that the prisoner had removed the nails and iron that secured his bunk to the wall so that he could expose it. Because the cell next to Reinhardt's was unoccupied, the jailers believed he was going to break through the wall, remove the window grate and then escape. Weighing four or five pounds, authorities considered that the iron might also be used as a weapon against the guards. It was also discovered that Pauline Dittmar and the prisoner were chatting through a corridor window where Reinhardt was allowed to walk for exercise. Apparently, Pauline climbed onto a barrel outside the window for their clandestine conversations. Pauline had not yet learned to avoid barrels where Edward Reinhardt was concerned.

The accused killer went on trial for the murder of his wife, Annie Degnan Reinhardt, on May 21, 1879. Newspapers called it "the most sensational of the many mysteries that have occurred on Staten Island within the past few years" and noted that it "excited the widest interest."[5] Well-known attorney Max Hubner defended Reinhardt, while Richmond County District Attorney John Croak prosecuted for the people. Held at the Richmond County Courthouse in the village of the same name, the twenty-two-year-old *Dandy Dutchman* wore a Prince Albert coat, closely buttoned; a Piccadilly collar; and cuffs that extended far below the coat sleeves.

Rosanna Degnan, along with Charles and Josephine Herborn, reiterated their inquest testimony, while a number of new witnesses were called. Richmond Turnpike (now Victory Boulevard) resident John Higgins described the man he saw pushing a wheelbarrow toward Silver Lake during July 1878. The description was an exact match to Reinhardt. An employee of the Cisco family, William Cummings, verified that he saw a stranger pushing a barrow up the same road at the same time. He told the man he was a "fool for not throwing that old barrow into the empty wagon which was ahead and so to save himself the trouble of wheeling it."[6] Dr. William Walser took the stand and shocked the courtroom by stating quite simply "that death had attended the act of giving birth to a child." Walser also announced that Annie's skull was fractured. Furthermore, he remarked that "the compression of the nerves at the base of the skull undoubtedly caused death within 15 minutes and prevented the woman from making any outcry or struggle. In the opinion of the Doctor, the blow which fractured the skull was struck while in the act of delivery, and was the only cause of death." When the defense objected, saying that he had examined a different skull than the one in the barrel, Dr. Walser replied, "I exhumed it myself; it is here at my feet." And with that, he pointed to a satchel beside his chair.[7]

The Richmond County Courthouse (left) and Jail in Richmond, the location of Reinhardt's trial, incarceration and execution. *From* History of Richmond County, Staten Island, *1887.*

The defense opened by attempting to advance the theory that "Reinhardt's wife was the victim of violent malpractice [abortion], to which he was not a party" and that "her body was concealed by him to hide the evidences of death, for he believed he would be charged with complicity, and he well knew the punishment that was imposed in such cases. His marriage with Pauline Dittmar was to atone for the act of seduction, which Reinhardt admitted." Amazingly, Reinhardt agreed that he buried the body of Annie Degnan at Silver Lake. With that, Reinhardt took the stand and announced that Annie took the 9:00 a.m. or 10:00 a.m. ferryboat to Manhattan on July 18, 1878, in order to see an unknown doctor. Returning at about 9:00 p.m., she stated that she had procured some medicine. At about 4:00 p.m. the next day, Annie complained of severe stomach pain after taking the prescription. Reinhardt claimed to have no idea why she took the medicine. Alleging that he had always treated her kindly and affectionately and that he never "struck her that night with a hammer and never inflicted a blow that would cause her death; she died between 11 and 12 o'clock." Reinhardt feared a charge of "criminal malpractice, and with having procured her death," so he concealed her body. He did acknowledge that testimony relating to him pushing the wheelbarrow with the barrel was correct, but he stated that his acts were to prevent finding her body in their quarters, "as circumstantial evidence would have been strong against me." Spectators, reporters, witnesses and the public called his testimony "sensational" and "extraordinary."[8] Much to everyone's surprise, and after a brief statement by Dr. Theodore Walser (William's father) that the girl's death could have been caused by any number of circumstances, the defense rested.

In closing, the prosecution stated that Reinhardt had motive to kill his wife. Firstly, he had two wives and as such was a bigamist, which was—and is— unlawful. Secondly, since the second wife wanted to establish housekeeping, the property owned by Annie Reinhardt—furniture, etc.—was needed for that purpose.

At 9:30 a.m. on May 23, 1879, the jury retired to deliberate. Returning in just forty minutes, it found the defendant guilty of murder in the first degree. The audience was said to be satisfied. Reinhardt expressed no emotion. Judge Dyckman asked if he had anything to say, to which he replied, "I did not murder Annie Degnan, or Mrs. Reinhardt, as they call her. She died from causes of taking medicine herself." Reinhardt then commenced a litany of complaints against the court, stating that he did not get a fair trial, that he did not see his lawyer often enough to get witnesses to clear him, that he was too poor to properly prepare a trial and that there was prejudice against him for being German. He blamed Annie's skull fracture on the barrel falling off the first wheelbarrow and degraded Annie by saying that she was not a "decent girl," that he initially met her in a dance hall and that he had spent that night with her. One audience member elicited a loud "hiss" when Reinhardt alleged that she often went to the doctor, insinuating that she had sought abortions in the past.[9]

Judge Dyckman announced that Edward Reinhardt would hang for the murder of Annie Degnan on July 11 between 9:00 a.m. and 2:00 p.m. at the Richmond County Jail. The defense immediately called for a stay of proceedings, which was granted, causing the punishment to be postponed for several months.

Pauline Dittmar was finally done with Reinhardt. Having stated at trial that she had demanded marriage to atone for the wrong he had committed—the wrong being unlawful physical relations before marriage—she called him a bad man and insisted she never wanted to lay eyes on him again. She was very concerned that a lasting stigma had been placed upon her reputation. It should be noted that the poor woman gave birth to his child on April 15, 1879.

January 9, 1880, was a sorrowful day for the Degnan family. Undertaker Daniel Dempsey removed Annie Degnan from the Poor House Potter's Field Cemetery so that she could be reinterred at Holy Cross Cemetery in Brooklyn. By this time, her remains consisted of not much more than

John J. Vaughan Jr. served as undersheriff at the Richmond County Jail during the confinement of Edward Reinhardt. *From Prominent Men of Staten Island, 1893.*

a mass of bones. When told that his wife was removed to Brooklyn for permanent interment, the disinterested Reinhardt said nothing more than "Is that so?" However, he did display emotion when fellow inmate John Larkin accused him of stealing jewelry. The resentful Reinhardt responded to the accusation by countering, "A man in my position don't much like being called a thief, especially if he is innocent. Now I found that jewelry lying on the floor in the corridor, and I held possession of it until I learned to whom it belonged." Undersheriff John J. Vaughan Jr. corroborated Reinhardt's story and stated that Larkin "frequently complained because he did not receive the same treatment as Reinhardt." According to Vaughan, "Larkin did not appear to understand the difference in position between himself and Eddy," owing to Eddy's notoriety.[10]

On February 10, 1880, the General Term of the Supreme Court upheld Reinhardt's conviction of murder, stating that there was abundant evidence given to the jury for the verdict. When told the news, Reinhardt threw himself on the jailhouse cot and wept. Reinhardt was now sentenced to be hanged from the gallows until dead on April 2.

Reinhardt was again busy with a jailbreak attempt, but a sheriff's deputy became wise to the effort when a letter from one of the prisoners was intercepted. It held ambiguous information on the breakout, but it did appear that they planned to dig through a wall of the jailhouse. The escape date also became apparent, and on that night, one of the convicts was twice found in a cell other than his own; meanwhile, Reinhardt opened his own cell with a homemade key.

Unobserved by officials, Reinhardt proceeded to free the two other prisoners, Owen Clark and James McGuirk (also known as "Mulligan's Ghost"). The three were finally discovered by watchmen at about 3:00 a.m.

Reinhardt drew, raised kittens, built miniature boats and planned his escape during imprisonment. *From the* National Police Gazette, *January 22, 1881.*

The key and other implements for the getaway were fashioned by Reinhardt, who amused himself by making toy boats and had thus accustomed his keepers to seeing him at work. For punishment, Clark and McGuirk were put in dark cells, while Reinhardt was denied use of the corridor for exercise and visitors. Complaining bitterly about the penalty, Reinhardt protested that it was natural for him to try and escape. As such, he could not understand why he should be punished. Displeasure and desperation were again displayed a month later, when he took the iron ball fastened to his leg and threw it at his cell door, breaking it. He claimed that he only wanted to show what could be done with the weighted implement, but in reality, Reinhardt believed his only salvation from the gallows would be fleeing the jail.

After further delays, Edward Reinhardt was sentenced to be hanged. By January 14, 1881, the gallows were to be completed at the Richmond Jail. The upcoming execution was causing quite a stir on Staten Island. From shore to shore, villages were abuzz with discussion on nothing else. No one had been hanged on Staten Island since the colonial era—almost one hundred years before! It seemed as if the entire population wanted to witness the hanging, but only those with an official pass from Sheriff Connor could attend. Many would be disappointed, as very few passes were distributed. To prevent observance of the event from outside the jail, a twelve-foot wall

Above: Edward Reinhardt relaxing with his cats and a smoke at the Richmond County Jail. *From the* National Police Gazette, *January 22, 1881.*

Left: Many women were intrigued with prisoner Reinhardt, and as such, he received many female visitors. *From the* National Police Gazette, *January 22, 1881.*

was erected. Reinhardt did receive several off-island visitors on January 10. They must have been very determined to get to the isolated lockup, as Staten Island ferries were completely off schedule, owing to magnificent ice cakes that floated in the harbor. The ice rammed against the hulls and clogged the great paddle wheels that moved the boats forward. After landing, it was then a seven-mile sleigh ride from the east shore to the county lockup, and this was through a blinding winter snowstorm!

Edward Reinhardt petitioned the governor for an additional ten days of life in order to "prepare to meet the creator of us all." Simply put, Reinhardt stated that he was not "prepared from a religious point of view," even though "he steadfastly rejected spiritual consolation and objected to the presence of ministers of the gospel in the jail" during his incarceration. It was also Reinhardt's contention that he was not born to hang.[11] In addition, his keepers kept a close eye that he did not attempt suicide. One fellow inmate noted that he would not be surprised if Reinhardt slit his own throat to avoid execution.

On January 10, 1881, the gallows of the Tombs Prison in Manhattan was removed and brought for reassembly to Staten Island to accommodate Edward Reinhardt, the "Silver Lake Murderer," also known as the "Dandy Dutchman." One paper noted, "The culprit to the last exhibited an amazing indifference to his fate and met his doom apparently as unmoved as if he were going to a matinee instead of to his death." Thousands of islanders descended on the little jail "and made it as much of a holiday as they would the Fourth of July." The island had not seen so much sensation in many a day. Two taverns outside the jail teemed with partygoers the evening before, with many a "smart popping of champagne corks and melodious laughter from ladies out with their escorts." The gaiety lasted until after midnight at one hotel and until daybreak at another. The festive sounds failed to pierce the walls of the jail, where Sheriff Connor was talking of Anthony Cornish's hanging for murder in 1789. In fact, Connor's father was one of the officials present at the execution. Three other lawmen were on hand to watch that Reinhardt did not kill himself. He chatted amiably with them and a few reporters from 8:00 p.m. until twenty minutes before 5:00 a.m. Also keeping him company were three cats that he had raised and cared for. One of the reporters described his "heavy, square jaw" as showing a "determined nature" and his "thick, sensuous lips denot[ing] powerful passions." His eyes were said to be "hard and cruel" with a frightening "wild light." At first, Reinhardt had a restless, melancholy air as he chain-smoked cigars provided by his visitors. The other inmates were said to be "nervous and uneasy." As the evening progressed, Reinhardt became more "disconsolate, hopeless, and utterly cast down" and then "fearful and nervous." Even so, he requested quail on toast for his last meal. The quail came with fried potatoes, bread and butter and coffee, but in the end, his appetite was lost and the food went uneaten. Interestingly, the quail had been carefully deboned so that he did not choke to death.[12]

Dressed in his trademark Prince Albert coat and Piccadilly collar with a purple scarf sporting white polka dots, Reinhardt at the last welcomed clergyman Reverend I.W. Brinkerhoff of the Tottenville Baptist Church. He insisted that he had not killed his wife and that she had died from an abortion, but even so, he told Brinkerhoff that he was ready to die.

The crowd started to arrive outside the jail at dawn. Onlookers marveled that the men of Staten Island must have all taken a holiday—farmers and fishermen, peddlers and politicians, storekeepers and sailors all arrived for the spectacle. The tavern keepers happily contemplated all the sandwiches, barrels of beer and "demijohns of firewater" that would be consumed that day. It was said that supplies were brought in all during the previous week and that the owners had even visited Manhattan to hire extra bartenders and drop off scores of invitations for the upcoming spectacle. Twenty police officers were on hand to control the crowd, and approximately one hundred special deputies were sworn in for the day's activities.

At 9:45 a.m., Sheriff Connor told Reinhardt it was time and began reading the record of Reinhardt's court proceedings. "The prisoner was then securely pinioned, the black cap was placed on his head and the Sheriff led him out to execution. As the doors to the jail yard were thrown open, Reinhardt was confronted by the gallows. The rain was falling heavily as the Rev. Mr. Brinkerhoff read the 23rd, 1st and 51st psalms." Onlookers yelled, "There! There he comes!" Brinkerhoff called for "divine mercy on the soul of the man about to die." When asked if he had anything to say, Reinhardt had no comment. As pelting rain began, the hangman took the noose that hung around Reinhardt's neck and attached it to the rope of the gallows. With that, the black cap was pulled down across his face. There was concern on the hangman's part, as the back of Reinhardt's head was on the same line with his vertebral column, and both were almost completely flat. The hangman feared that the noose would slip off the murderer's head. He need not have worried. At four minutes past 10:00 a.m., a weight was dropped and Reinhardt was quickly drawn into the air. There was much struggle—kicking and spasmodic movement of the body—so much so that a number of onlookers were moved to tears. After hanging for approximately fifteen minutes, the corpse was lowered and three physicians officially pronounced Reinhardt dead. The remains were released to his sister, and he was buried at Silver Mount Cemetery, which, interestingly, is directly across from Silver Lake. Neither Reinhardt's family nor the family of his murdered wife attended the execution. One observant woman was overheard to remark that Reinhardt deserved "the stretching" he got that day.

Several days after the execution, a number of individuals visited the jail to buy the items crafted by Reinhardt. These included a steamship, two schooners, four full-rigged ships, a pilot boat, several propellers and a number of fancy canes. Several small yet detailed ships were even built in soda-water bottles. The visitors were disappointed to discover that they could not purchase anything, as Reinhardt's mother and sister had visited two days before his hanging and removed all of his personal belongings. One of the schooners was actually attached to the wall in Sheriff Connor's office.

It seems that Edward Reinhardt was not done with Staten Island even after his hanging. On the evening of March 14, 1881, undertaker Daniel Dempsey swore that he saw the ghostly visage of the wife murderer resting his hand on a wheelbarrow that held a barrel with cut staves along the Richmond Turnpike. Dempsey was terrified, as was his horse, which plunged violently at the encounter. Dempsey had been the undertaker in charge of Annie Degnan's body after its discovery, and his brother had been the investigating coroner into her murder. Dempsey even made a legal affidavit that the apparition he witnessed was that of Edward Reinhardt. Four other individuals, prominent in the Staten Island community, went to investigate. Much to their surprise, they saw the man with the barrow near Cebra Avenue and the Richmond Turnpike. When they began chasing him, the ghost literally flew away. One of these witnesses, John Rooney, also swore out an affidavit that the apparition was Edward Reinhardt. Needless to say, the Turnpike became quite deserted at night—except for ghost-hunters.

But whatever became of Ellen Murphy? Indeed, she was amongst the living. Ellen appeared in Clifton around the end of October 1878, stating that she had been in Manhattan. While in dispose, she had heard of the mysterious body in the barrel at Silver Lake; the arrest of her lover, Louis Reige, for questioning in her disappearance; and of Louis's subsequent release—all of which prompted her return, but none too quickly of course. She did arrive with a healthy baby in her arms. Louis Reige was overjoyed by their homecoming, and he immediately asked her to marry him.

Chapter 2
DEAD AMONG THE ROCKS

A Protestant prayer book, two black beaded bracelets, a pin and an unusual gold ring set with a "cat's eye" were found on the body. Discovered by Thomas Armour, the janitor of the Clifton Boat Club, he first thought it was a log but soon realized it was human! Retrieving the body from the water's rocky edge was fortunate, as many who fell (or were thrown) into the New York Harbor simply washed out into the Atlantic Ocean, never to be seen again. Armour made this awful discovery on Sunday, May 12, 1889.

Identified by Dr. Samuel A. Robinson of West New Brighton, the dead woman was Mary E. Tobin, who had been employed as his office assistant until April 13, 1889. At the time, Miss Tobin stated she was off for an extended visit to her Franklin, Pennsylvania family. She was thrilled to tell all that she would be married upon her return. It was odd though—most people had no idea who she was marrying. Some thought he was a well-off New York City stockbroker, while others believed he was a Staten Island resident. Before her trip, Mary told Dr. Robinson she would be visiting Mrs. Frank McKinney in Long Island City. After the visit, Mary returned for another goodbye to the doctor's office on Monday, April 15, 1889. Before she left Robinson, Mary took one of the doctor's ledgers, stating that she would update it with several addresses. In case it was misplaced, Robinson took the opportunity to wrap the book in brown paper and label it with his name and address. With that, Mary expressed two trunks—one to Franklin and one to Mrs. McKinney—and was gone to Pennsylvania. This turned out to be an assumption on everyone's part.

Top: Dr. Samuel Robinson identified the body of Mary Tobin after it washed up at Clifton. *From* History of Richmond County, Staten Island, *1887*.

Bottom: Even though Mary Tobin was a complex woman, no one believed she committed suicide. *From* The World, *May 27, 1889*.

A few days later, Mrs. McKinney arrived at Robinson's office concerned that she had received Mary's trunk, but Mary had not stopped to get it. Then, in early May, Miss Tobin's brothers, Daniel and David, came to Robinson's office inquiring about her whereabouts.

The mystery of Mary's whereabouts was finally solved when a Mrs. Dixon of Jersey City, New Jersey (Mary's aunt), heard about the body found on Staten Island's shoreline. She went directly to the Stapleton Morgue to make inquiries and was shown the jewelry found on the dead woman. Sadly, she identified it as belonging to Mary. According to Mrs. Dixon, Mary was despondent during her last visit. When asked if she had any troubles, Mary responded, "Oh, no. It's just a fancy of mine."

By order of Coroner Martin Hughes, Dr. John Feeney, health officer for the Town of Middleton, performed an autopsy on the dead woman. He refused to share the results until the onset of an inquest. Feeney was also awaiting results from pathology expert Dr. H.P. Loomis of the University of the City of New York, who was studying body parts and organs sent by Feeney.

As the mystery unfolded, there was vast speculation as to how Mary Tobin ended up dead. When asked if her fiancé knew of her demise, most people vaguely shook their heads since no one knew his identity. In fact, no one recalled seeing her with any man other than Dr. Samuel Robinson or his son. One clue showed that Mary went to the Bard Avenue medical office of Dr. William J. Bryan after leaving Dr. Robinson's on April 15. When she departed, Bryan walked her to the Livingston train station. This turned out to be the last time Mary Tobin was seen alive…or was it? When interviewed, Bryan refused to discuss whether he was the elusive fiancé. But one thing was certain: Bryan and Mary had become—and remained—close after he departed as junior physician from Dr. Robinson's practice. Oftentimes thereafter, Mary visited his new office.

It caused a profound sensation when Mrs. Horace Hillyer announced that she saw Mary Tobin alive and well on April 29, the day of the great naval parade. The wife of a well-known grocer, Hillyer claimed to know Mary, as she was a patient of Dr. Robinson's. She said that Miss Tobin was with a woman and child on a road between Livingston and West New Brighton. Seeing Miss Tobin struck her as strange since she heard that Mary had left the island.

Another sighting put Mary Tobin on the 8:30 p.m. Staten Island ferry from Saint George to Whitehall on May 3. It came from Harry the Trapeze Artist, who claimed to have seen a distressed Mary Tobin at the bow of a boat. After turning to toss his cigar over the side of the ferry, he looked back to discover that she was gone. It was his belief that "Mary" had jumped overboard.

One outlandish theory had Mary walking along the trestlework of the north shore railroad by Sailors' Snug Harbor on Richmond Terrace after Dr. Bryan left the train station. Rumor had it that she missed her footing, fell into the Kill Van Kull and drowned. This theory was based on the fact that Mary's clothing was saturated with an oily acidic film similar to one that

Left: Mary Tobin's fiancé, Dr. William Bryan. *From* The World, *May 27, 1889.*

Below: The Bard Avenue residence and office of Dr. Bryan and the Livingston Train Station where Mary Tobin was last seen. *From* Robinson's Atlas, *1907.*

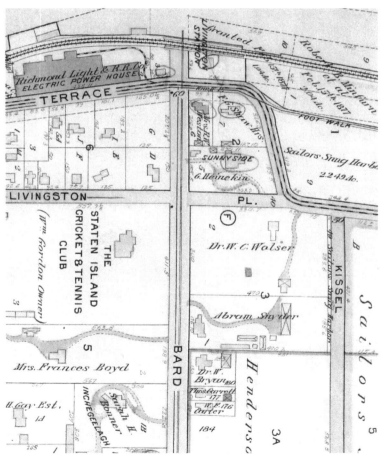

accumulated near Snug Harbor, owing to effluence from the Standard Oil Works at Bayonne and Constable Hook, New Jersey.

The mysterious disappearance took another turn when Dr. Robinson's wrapped ledger was returned by a young lad the day after Miss Tobin took it for updating. According to Robinson, the boy who left it ran off so quickly he could not get his name or the name of who sent the package.

Mary Tobin had begun her employment with Dr. Robinson two years earlier, during April 1887. As his office assistant and a resident of Robinson's household, Mary became very attached to the doctor's father, who also lived in the house. According to the doctor, Mary had few office skills, but since his father was fond of her and she took good care of him, Robinson kept her on. Describing her as calm and stoical, Robinson believed Mary would never do "anything contrary to her own inclinations." He did acknowledge that she exhibited some curious religious transformations. A devout Methodist, Mary attended Trinity Methodist Church regularly. Owing to an unknown controversy at the church, she "became a rank infidel" and switched to being a "High Church Episcopalian" at Saint Mary's Episcopal Church on Castleton Avenue in West New Brighton.[13] In 1888, Mary began investigating the Episcopalian sisterhood. Robinson believed her interest faded, owing to the impending marriage. When asked to identify her fiancé, Robinson refused to divulge that information, saying only that Mary often spoke of his fine beard and moustache. Robinson bluntly added that he never really liked the woman. It also came to light that Mary sometimes left Dr. Robinson's early in the evening and remained away all night.

Owing to Mary Tobin's strong personality, no one believed she committed suicide. Most thought she met her end by foul play. Of course, all of West New Brighton and the surrounding communities were discussing the mysterious death. Because the authorities had little to say on the subject, suspense mounted. The heightened discussion was enflamed by the Tobin family's slow effort in directly identifying or claiming the body. Coroner Hughes plainly stated that if they did not collect her remains soon, they would find them buried, owing to health regulations.

One theory put forth by Coroner Gorman of the Southfield section of Staten Island was that Mary Tobin died from carbolic acid poisoning and was thrown into the harbor at Red Hook, Brooklyn. Why he should say such a thing no one knew, especially since he had no involvement with the autopsy or inquest, nor had he viewed or studied the body. It seemed everyone had an opinion.

The identity of the mystery fiancé was finally clarified by Mrs. Frank McKinney. It was Dr. William J. Bryan. Described as a fine-looking athletic

Coroner Martin Hughes presided over the inquests into Mary Tobin's death. *From Prominent Men of Staten Island, 1893.*

man with pleasant manners, Bryan was approximately thirty years old. A reporter for *The World* who met with Dr. Bryan on May 15 stated that the doctor did not "have the appearance of a lover mourning the untimely fate of his sweetheart. In fact, he seemed quite jovial and during the conversation frequently gave vent to laughter." (Dr. Bryan would later deny that he was lighthearted during this interview.) When asked if he was Mary Tobin's fiancé, Bryan became grave and evasively replied, "I don't care to say anything in answer to that question." He did admit to being the last person to see Mary Tobin alive (since many thought Mrs. Horace Hillyer was mistaken). Stating that he had no patience for the theory that Mary committed suicide, he acknowledged that she might have accidentally fallen off a ferry. Bryan also noted that bad feelings existed between him and Dr. Robinson, with the latter believing that the younger physician opened his practice far too close to Robinson's office. In response to Robinson's dislike of Mary, Bryan said that the older man liked only money and that with the death of Robinson's father, the home was no longer "congenial" to Mary.[14] Bryan further noted that a dispute ensued between Mary and Robinson because the doctor owed her money. Robinson denied the allegation.

The inquest into Mary Tobin's untimely death took place on May 16, 1889, at the Rosebank funeral home owned by Coroner Hughes. Following testimony from Janitor Armour on finding the washed-up body, Mary Tobin's brother David made a statement. Then Dr. Bryan took the stand. Wearing French, trimmed spectacles and perfect attire, Dr. Bryan stated that he had last seen Mary at his office on April 15 between 8:00 p.m. and 9:00 p.m. They chatted for twenty minutes. During their talk, Bryan received an urgent phone call regarding a house visit, so Mary took her leave, saying that she was headed to Mrs. McKinney's that evening. As such, Bryan walked Mary to the Livingston train station and then returned to his office. Thereafter, he left for the house call. Returning at about midnight, he found the brown paper–covered package addressed to Dr. Robinson. Realizing that Robinson would not be happy with it in his hands, he expressed the package to the senior doctor with the young lad. Dr. Bryan first heard of Miss Tobin's death via a dispatch from her brother. Coroner Hughes was about to excuse Bryan from the stand when the doctor abruptly announced that he and Mary were engaged to be married.

Dr. John Feeney performed the autopsy on Mary Tobin's body. *From* Prominent Men of Staten Island, *1893.*

Dr. John L. Feeney then took the stand and revealed that the young woman was not poisoned. No, her death was caused by asphyxia. He hastily added that the postmortem was not complete.

Pathologist Dr. H.P. Loomis reported that the body had been in the water for approximately eight to ten days before it was found on the Clifton shoreline. This belief left several days during which Miss Tobin was missing and unaccounted for. Loomis further noted that no evidence had been found to indicate any criminal operation (abortion) was performed or that Miss Tobin was pregnant. Loomis proclaimed Miss Tobin as "pure."[15] This was a positive development for Bryan, who many believed was the cause of her demise. Later, Robinson would declare that Mary Tobin was not a virgin when she died, with Dr. Feeney responding that "such an assertion is an outrage upon decency and good sense." Feeney further accused Robinson of a "breech of good taste in casting the terrible slur."[16]

Railroad ticket agent Miss McTammany swore under oath that Mary Tobin did not pass the ticket booth the night she was last seen. She was well acquainted with Mary, as she often left packages and umbrellas for the ticket agent to watch.

So many inquisitive spectators showed up for the second night of the inquest that Coroner Hughes moved it to Kattenmeier's Hall on Saint Mary's Avenue in Rosebank. Here Dr. Samuel Robinson took the stand. He stated that he had last seen Mary Tobin on April 15. At that time, she was cheerful, and he did not believe for even one second that she had taken her own life.

Mrs. McKinney then testified that Mary always wore a "chamois skin pouch" under her clothing. The pouch contained a picture of Dr. Bryan, her address and some money. All were surprised when Coroner Hughes noted that the body did not bear such a pouch, that her outfit was buttoned to the throat and that absolutely no money had been found on the body.

During this time, Mary's remains were finally returned to Pennsylvania. They were so decomposed that a special airtight metallic casket was needed. The burial was to take place on May 19, 1889.

On May 20, Dr. Bryan was questioned about the medical call he made on the night Mary disappeared. Discussion included the fact that Bryan left Mary at the station before the train arrived since she wanted him to make his call quickly and get home because he was not feeling well. As such, he headed back to his office, where Timothy McInerney drove him to the home of Mr. E.J. Field in Willow Brook. A reporter investigating the timing of the events of April 15 noted a discrepancy. According to the doctor, he left Miss Tobin at the train station at 8:54 p.m. and arrived at the Field home about twenty minutes before 11:00 p.m. Why did it take one hour and forty minutes to hitch the horse and drive a distance that should have been covered in thirty minutes by carriage ride? This led many to ponder Bryan's whereabouts, but when McInerney was called to the stand, he stated that three other house calls were made prior to arriving at the Field house.

On May 22, Dr. Feeney was called back and again testified that death had been caused by asphyxia from drowning and that he had found no evidence of foul play. The report of Dr. Loomis was then read, with the conclusion that the heart and stomach were normal, with no evidence of disease, poisoning or chemicals. A Mrs. W.J. Hasbrouck also took the stand, and like Mrs. Hillyer, she claimed to have seen Mary Tobin on the day of the naval parade.

The inquest brought only further questions and theories. Did Mary Tobin really disappear on April 15, or did she drown at a later date? Why wouldn't Coroner Hughes allow Coroner Wood to testify? Wood was very vocal in his belief that Mary was killed before she entered the water since no water was found in her stomach, but he was not asked to speak at the inquest. Owing to these questions, another inquest was held on May 27, 1889, with Dr. Robinson echoing Wood's belief that Mary Tobin did not drown. It should be noted that Robinson was at both autopsies. For his part, Doctor Loomis would not be held to any singular cause of death. A number of other witnesses took the stand, but little was added by their testimony. At 11:00 p.m., Hughes called an adjournment whereby Dr. Wood stood and asked to make an affidavit confirming the statements of Dr. Robinson. Hughes gruffly replied that it was too late—there was no time left that evening. Wood asked if he would be allowed to make a statement at the next hearing, to which Hughes replied, "Well, maybe if I have time, I will allow you."[17]

Another hearing was held on June 4, 1889. Dr. Wood and Dr. Robinson both testified, but nothing new was revealed, so Coroner Hughes adjourned the inquest indefinitely. He was very unhappy with the medical community and complained that they made the task of reaching a conclusion very difficult. A final hearing did take place on July 3, 1889. After two hours of deliberation, the jury declared that

J. Walter Wood, MD. Dr. Wood fervently believed that Mary Tobin was alive when she entered the water. *From* Prominent Men of Staten Island, *1893.*

Mary had died of asphyxia—the cause of which was unknown.

Perhaps Dr. Bryan had upset Mary by breaking off their engagement that last night he saw her. Others wondered if the Wall Street stockbroker was another attachment who complicated matters between the two. Many questioned why the district attorney was not involved with the case. But what surprised most was Hughes's overall handling of the inquest. *The World* referred to the inquest as a "stupid investigation" and declared that the local newspapers had discovered more facts than the coroner. The publication further wrote, "Evidence steadily points to the conclusion that Mary Tobin was murdered and her lifeless body cast into the silent waters of the harbor to be mangled into an unrecognizable mass by the paddle-wheels of the ferry-boats." It referred to "police imbecility" when describing the authority's response to the woman's death and asked whether law enforcement had "lost their wits." Police Chief Blake admitted, "I know nothing. I am a perfect ignoramus in this case." Others called Coroner Hughes "testy" and noted that he even neglected to bring a stenographer to document testimony.[18] Instead, he took the notes himself and even quieted jurors who attempted to ask questions.

According to Staten Island's upper echelon, as a rising young physician, Dr. Bryan's connection with Mary Tobin's mysterious demise did not complement him or his career. Many were surprised when he announced their engagement, since it was believed he "would have looked higher for an alliance." Further damage was done in the summer of 1889, when a Watertown, New York newspaper charged that Dr. Bryan and a woman known only as the "Lady in Black" had "improper relations" while she lived in West New Brighton. When the story broke with her true identity, Mrs. Korleen Fowler was prominently highlighted in several newspapers throughout the state. Her father, Anson Moore, a well-known New York City lawyer, promised a lawsuit against the newspaper that first published the story. Moore argued that the announcement contained "not an atom of truth." One of the most damaging charges was that Mrs. Fowler and Dr. Bryan had spent several days alone together in Ontario. The article also intimated "that Dr. Bryan and she entered into a conspiracy to kill her husband in order that they could be married." Bryan and Mrs. Fowler met in 1883, when her father bought a house in West New Brighton. Mrs. Fowler stayed in the house to care for her sick mother, who was being treated by Dr. Bryan. Fowler eventually returned to Watertown, New York, but after her husband, Colonel Charles B. Fowler, died on April 13, 1889, she moved back to West New Brighton. Eyebrows were raised at the timing of Fowler's death and the disappearance of Mary Tobin. Suspicion was further aroused when it became known that the first person to hear of Colonel Fowler's death was Dr. Bryan. It seems Mrs. Fowler went so far as to telegraph him the very same evening the colonel died. Rumors were soon cast about that Fowler died under "peculiar circumstances."[19] It also appears that gossip about the "woman in black" and Dr. Bryan had already caused dissention between Mary and Dr. Bryan.

The Mary Tobin murder mystery had commenced fading from the public's radar when a ghastly event summoned it back to the headlines. At 5:00 a.m. on May 23, 1891, the Franklin Fire Department was called to the Pennsylvania house of Mary's father. Home alone, N.P. Tobin's dead body was found among the fire-scarred ruins. But it was not the fire that killed Mr. Tobin. His head was lying in a pool of blood, and there was a sizeable bruise above his eyes. Furthermore, he had been choked to death. Fingernail impressions were still visible on the dead man's throat. A powerful and active man, it appeared that numerous assailants had taken Tobin down. Tools found on the scene verified that murderers had broken into the house. Many believed Tobin was killed because he knew the identity of the person who took his daughter's life. Tobin had no enemies; as a matter of fact, he was known for aiding the poor and even prisoners. Some thought it was a murder to hide a murder!

It was suggested that Dr. Samuel Robinson knew something about Tobin's murder and as such traveled to Franklin to discuss the situation with authorities. On arrival, he proclaimed that Mary Tobin was murdered. He claimed that the investigation into her death was stymied and stifled and that her body was not in the water the entire time that she was missing. Robinson believed she was concealed somewhere on Staten Island during this period. Robinson further commented on the conduct of Dr. Bryan at the autopsy. He believed the man was heartless, and he recalled with a shudder that Dr. Bryan and Mary were engaged. Stating that the Tobin family had turned against him, Robinson believed they were circulating a rumor that he was Mary's assassin. The May 8, 1891 edition of *The World* reported, "The authorities at Franklin, Pennsylvania firmly believe that Tobin was murdered in order to prevent him from coming to this city, as he had expressed an intention to do, for the purpose of investigating more thoroughly his daughter's death. They think that the same person or persons who were responsible for his daughter's death have been instrumental in putting him out of the way."[20]

In Franklin, Pennsylvania, there were now two sides regarding the murder of Mary Tobin: the Bryanites and the Robinsonites. Each professed that their man was the innocent victim of outrageous persecution while the other doctor was a cold-blooded killer.

Dr. Bryan firmly reiterated that he lacked any knowledge of Mary Tobin's death. He went on to note that Robinson flew into rages in front of Mary and that he vowed to have Bryan driven from his Staten Island practice. Mary so feared these outbreaks that she had suggested they end the engagement, but Bryan would not hear of it. Robinson continued to insinuate that Dr. Bryan's money, and the money of his friends, was used to stifle the inquiry in 1889. One Staten Island resident reported that an anti-Bryan faction had formed with talk abounding about the coroner purchasing $2,000 worth of costly Staten Island property after the inquest.

The situation was further complicated during mid-May 1891, when Dr. Bryan's former housekeeper, Mrs. W.S. Glassford, came forward to discuss Dr. Bryan and his relationship with Mary Tobin. Of the doctor, she charged that he was not the suave gentleman that people perceived. Furthermore, she called Miss Tobin's actions "unmaidenly" and noted that she often spent the whole evening "behind closed doors" with Dr. Bryan. According to Glassford, the couple would move a chaise lounge in front of the door so no one could enter. Mary would "stay far into the night" and sometimes not leave until half-past twelve, "and then she would sneak out of the house and walk back to Dr. Robinson's alone or else take the last Shore Road horsecar back." Both Bryan's office assistant and Mrs. Glassford were "scandalized" by the behavior. Glassford also said that Bryan was guilty of "impropriety." She swore that when Mary and Bryan walked to the train station on April 15, Mary was weeping uncontrollably. Glassford believed Mary was "frantic" over the telegram Dr. Bryan received from Mrs. Fowler about her husband's death. According to Mrs. Glassford, Dr. Bryan was seen with Mrs. Fowler just two weeks later: "They were laughing and talking and seemed delighted with each other's company." When confronted with her allegations, Bryan denied them and said he would "make her smart for the lies she has uttered." Calling her bitter and unhappy, he accused her of making these charges owing to his complaints about how she ran his household. Furthermore, she owed him and untold numbers of Staten Island tradesmen money. "I shall follow her now to the bitter end and force her to prove what she says or suffer."[21] On May 15, 1891, Dr. Bryan went to District Attorney Thomas Fitzgerald insisting that he reopen the examination into Mary Tobin's death. "He courted the fullest investigation and defied anyone to prove the stories which had appeared in public print about him lately."[22]

As if two deaths didn't bring enough misery for one family, the Tobin's suffered yet another tragedy on September 28, 1891, when an arsonist set fire to the tin shop of Kincaid and Tobin. There was no doubt that it was arson, as a man was seen running from the blaze. It was D.S. Tobin's opinion that "some enemy of the family is at the bottom of all the trouble, and may not stop, unless unmasked, until the entire family is wiped out of existence."[23]

No one ever solved the mysterious death of Mary Tobin or the death of her father, or even the destruction by fire of her brother's tin shop. Dr. William Bryan would go on to have a successful career as a physician on Staten Island. Active in the community, he participated with the Staten Island Cricket and Baseball Club, the Staten Island Whist Club, the Masons, the Richmond County Country Club and the Richmond County Automobile Club. On April 18, 1900, he married Mary A. Rawson, the daughter of former district attorney Sydney Rawson. Bryan was prominently featured in the society pages of the newspapers as supporting and attending many charity events for the S.R. Smith Infirmary (later Staten Island Hospital). Chief of staff at the hospital for twenty years, Bryan died of heart disease at the age of seventy-two on February 25, 1932. The funeral was held at his residence at 91 Bard Avenue.

Dr. Samuel A. Robinson as he looked toward the close of the nineteenth century. *From* A Memorial History of Staten Island, *1898.*

Dr. Robinson's career was marred when he was taken to court by the relatives of Mrs. Levinia Van Emburg in 1892. The woman's nephew, Alexander W. Farrell, accused Robinson of exerting undue influence over his aunt to such an extent that she altered her will to give him the bulk of her estate. As such, when she died, Robinson was the recipient of and/or controlled approximately $200,000. Robinson asserted that Van Emburg was an invalid and that he cared for her in his home with employed nurses for the last four years of her life. Furthermore, he claimed to have once been engaged to her daughter, who had predeceased her mother.

His opponents claimed that he had convinced Mrs. Van Emburg that no one could successfully combat her illness—that he was the only one who understood illnesses of the nervous type. Mrs. Van Emburg died at the Robinson residence, 163 Richmond Terrace, on January 10, 1892. Witnesses did come forward to say that Mrs. Van Emburg had complained about Robinson's power and actions over her, that she was unhappy with the will and that she had unsuccessfully asked him for an accounting of her finances. Even so, the judge ruled that the will go to probate as it stood, thus allowing Dr. Robinson to collect a financial windfall.

Chapter 3
A WICKED LOVE

It was scandalous! Kate Owens lived with a man without benefit of marriage. Many thought she got what she deserved when her lover, Edward Emmons, shot and killed her on the evening of October 24, 1890. After putting four bullets into Kate, Emmons made a halfhearted attempt at his own life by glancing a bullet off his brow. Largely unsuccessful at anything he attempted in life, the shot created only a flesh wound.

Prior to living with Emmons, Kate had been married to Charles Owens. Only a short time after the nuptials, Kate discovered that Owens had a wife and children in Connecticut, so she left him. Eventually, she again met Edward Emmons, and they moved in together. They had actually known each other since childhood, and he had always loved her. Emmons came from a good family. His brother was a ferryboat pilot on the *Robert Garrett*, and his father worked for Bayley A. Emmons, a family owned leather dealer in Manhattan. Young Emmons was a clerk in this company until approximately 1887. After that time, he did not work, instead drinking most days until drunk. Claiming to have saved her from a degraded life, Emmons called Kate unfaithful and ungrateful for the care he provided. For six years, they lived at 20 New York Avenue in Clifton, but a short time before the murder, they separated, with Emmons miserably moving to a room at the nearby Vanderbilt House. Claiming to have obtained a job in Saint Louis, he asked Kate if he could see her one last time before his departure. Perhaps he could convince her to join him.

When Emmons arrived, Kate's fifteen-year-old brother, George Wagenstein, and his friend August Scheidlemantle were visiting. The boys

GEORGE MARTIN'S
Vanderbilt ✦ House,

CLIFTON, STATEN ISLAND.

———— • ————

Lodging by the Day or Week.

———— • ————

The Larder Always Stocked with the Best,
The Bar with the Choicest.

———— • ————

MEALS AT ALL HOURS.

Asked to leave the home of Kate Owens, Edward Emmons moved into the Vanderbilt House in Clifton. *From* An Illustrated Sketchbook of Staten Island, *1886.*

would later state that the meeting started out almost pleasantly until Emmons asked Kate about ferryman James Vines. It was his belief that the two had been together the evening before. He also accused her of intimacies with brewer Joseph Rubsam of the Rubsam and Horrmann Atlantic Brewery. Kate denied Vines's visit and promptly told Emmons to leave. As he did, he requested that they shake hands, since he did not want to leave on an unharmonious note. When she refused, he flew into a rage, pulled out a seven-chamber revolver and fired five times in rapid succession. Four bullets entered her body. The last severed Kate's jugular vein, causing her to bleed to death. Emmons fled the building, with George yelling, "Murderer!" whereupon two men grabbed the killer. Emmons was subsequently locked up. He claimed to not remember having shot Kate, but he did hope the wounds were not fatal.

Edward Emmons's deed was called cowardly by some, while others defended Kate for putting him out for his drunken idleness. A reporter visited the scene the following day and actually found Kate's iced remains under a glass-lid coffin. He wrote, "Her features…showed that she must have been a beautiful woman in life. The room showed that she was a neat housekeeper, and the engravings on the walls and the bric-a-brac artistically arranged about the apartment were evidence of refinement."[24] Basins of wash were observed. It seems Kate took in laundry when she could not make ends meet as a dressmaker.

George Wagenstein informed authorities that three weeks before the execution, Emmons had sworn Kate would either marry him or die. When Wagenstein questioned her about marrying Emmons, she said she could not unless he gave up drinking.

District Attorney Thomas Fitzgerald ordered Kate's murdered body and the surrounding apartment photographed. Staten Island's most well-known photographer of the day, Isaac Almstaedt, was called in. Following a funeral service at her New York Avenue home on October 27, 1890, Kate was laid to rest in Silver Mount Cemetery in Silver Lake.

Edward Emmons's trial began on January 12, 1891. Judge J.F. Barnard presided. Emmons was defended by former Richmond County district attorney George W. Gallagher. Emmons's elderly father and two sisters were in the courtroom, as was revivalist Mrs. Lillian Van Dunn. Mrs. Dunn was credited with keeping Emmons from a breakdown. Throughout the trial, she sat by him and whispered words of encouragement. Since there was no dispute that Emmons had shot and killed Kate Owens, the defense hoped to prove that he had been temporarily deranged at the time of the murder, while the prosecution persisted that the murder had been premeditated and deliberate. On the witness stand, George Wagenstein stated that three weeks before the murder, Kate had sworn out an order for Emmons's arrest. She hoped it would prevent him from disturbing her. Witnesses at the murder scene testified that before he was carted off to jail, Emmons wanted to kiss Kate's face as she lay dead on the apartment floor.

After five hours of deliberation on January 15, 1891, Emmons was found guilty of murder in the second degree. Judge Barnard sentenced him to life imprisonment at Sing Sing. Given Emmons's past history and his statement that he preferred death to life imprisonment, Sheriff John Elsworth put a permanent guard on Emmons in case he attempted suicide again. On January 16, 1891, Elsworth took Emmons to Sing Sing. This was not the last time anyone would hear of Kate Owen's murderer.

The Sun, one of New York City's most prolific newspapers, reported on November 8, 1891, that Edward Emmons's father had obtained a pardon

Left: District Attorney Thomas Fitzgerald prosecuted and won the murder trial of Edward Emmons. *From* Prominent Men of Staten Island, *1893.*

Below: Staten Island's leading photographer, Isaac Almstaedt, was asked to photograph the crime scene of Kate Owen's murder. *From* An Illustrated Sketchbook of Staten Island, *1886.*

Almstaedt

INSTANTANEOUS

PORTRAIT AND LANDSCAPE

❖ Photographer, ❖

Tompkinsville, Staten Island.

Publisher of Photographs of Staten Island Scenery.

Telephone Call, 48 D.

by petitioning New York State governor David B. Hill. Supposedly, Emmons had consumption, better known now as tuberculosis, and would soon be dead from the disease hence he should be set free. It was noted at the time that Emmons's father was quite influential in the city and the state. Even so, the report was vehemently denied by Sing Sing warden William R. Brown, who said Emmons was not dying and was attending to his business as a shipping clerk in the prison clothing department. Oddly enough, ten years later, Edward Emmons did walk out of Sing Sing Prison a free man. Pardoned by then-governor Benjamin B. O'Dell Jr., he was released on June 12, 1901, at the request of General and Mrs. Edwin A. McAlpin. According to one report, a number of influential people worked on Emmons's behalf, including former judge Barnard, prosecuting district attorney Thomas Fitzgerald, Superintendant of Prisons Cornelius R. Collins and a woman known as Mrs. Maude Booth. While imprisoned, Emmons was involved with the Sing Sing branch of the Volunteer Prison League, an organization founded by Ballington and Maude Booth. The forerunner of the Volunteers of America, the Volunteer Prison League brought Christianity to the incarcerated and strove to be a positive and inspirational force to give prisoners hope. Residences for released prisoners were established, and the league also reached out to assist the families of prisoners. Branches were established at Dannemora and Auburn in New York State, San Quentin and Folsom in California and Walla Walla in Washington. The league eventually expanded throughout the country.

Upon his release, Emmons was driven to the Ossining train station by General McAlpin himself. From there, it was said that he went to his home at Staten Island. A 1903 report claims that Emmons lived and worked successfully in South America. In a position of high trust, he was doing very well financially. It seems that Edward Emmons was a successful "graduate" of Mrs. Booth's Volunteer Prison League—but what of Kate Owens?

Chapter 4
THE GREAT TOTTENVILLE MYSTERY

I t was a horrific discovery. A man had sliced his throat with his own shaving razor and lay dead on the floor of the Astor House in Manhattan. Found on February 3, 1891, there was nothing on the body or in the hotel room to identify the man. All labels had been sliced out of his clothes. There were no letters, a passport or anything else to provide his name. While having signed in as Fred Evans of England, no one believed this to be his identity. There was a well-known spiritualist named Fred Evans in the United States, but he lived in San Francisco. Said to have great powers, this Fred Evans had just returned from a successful tour of Australia.

The dead man was described as delicate and small framed with the tiny hands of a gentleman, a limp mustache and curly sandy-brown hair. He also had a prominent beak-like nose and thin lips. In some manner, he did resemble the famed spiritualist. When found, he was clad only in brown woolen underclothing. An interesting aspect of the suicide was that the victim did not cut his throat in the way that most do. Usually, one cuts straight across the windpipe, not the jugular, thus creating a horrific mess. This victim made three deep, neat cuts on the left side of the neck, thus doing the job correctly and tidily.

All manner of individuals attempted to put a name on the deceased. Frederick B. Altman of Birmingham, Alabama, arrived at the undertaking to see if the man was the Fred Evans who managed a plantation in Havana, Cuba. The dead man bore a resemblance, so Altman promised to cable Havana to see if his Fred Evans was alive and well. A woman from Boston

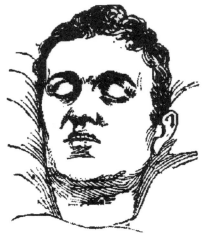

Above: The Astor House as it appeared in earlier years. *From* Treat's Illustrated New York: Brooklyn and Surroundings, *1874.*

Left: An 1891 drawing of the dead "Fred Evans," later identified as William Wright. *From the* Auburn Bulletin, *March 27, 1891.*

ventured in to see if he was a portrait painter she knew. She agreed to return with a friend who also knew the artist. Two other women appeared and identified the body as that of Fred Edgar. They claimed he was the nephew of a man who killed himself at the Getty House in Yonkers. They offered to bury him next to his uncle, whose last name was also Edgar, but they never returned to claim the body. They also never gave their names, real or stage, as they claimed to be actors. This is how they knew of the Getty House suicide, as Fred Edgar was also an actor. Soon, there was an entire circus surrounding the dead man as being a member of the Edgar family. It was orchestrated by charlatan Perrin H. Sumner, who made a practice of falsely asserting to know the names of abandoned suicide victims. As such, he became known as the "Great Identifier." This activity started as early as 1866. The majority of his identifications were that of a mythical Englishman with the last name Edgar. No one ever discovered why he pursued this activity or what the Edgar connection was. During his lifetime, he would be convicted of assaulting a woman, stock fraud, forgery, perjury and various real estate offenses. On June 14, 1907, he married elderly landlady Auguste Sommerkern, who had acquired a hefty sum for her golden years, on her deathbed. Ten days after the marriage, she died and her family brought a number of suits against Perrin and his son for swindling the woman.

So, Perrin H. Sumner jumped into the "Fred Evans" mix, further confusing the identification process of the Astor House suicide. However, his claim that both the Astor House suicide and the Getty House suicide were Edgars was finally nullified. No doubt the two actresses were somehow connected to Sumner's activities.

Since no one requested the body, Coroner Levy called for the burial of "Fred Evans" at the Potter's Field of Hart Island with the understanding that if anyone came forward, it would be turned over to the proper claimant. February 1891 closed without the lifeless man identified. He was interred at the Potter's Field on March 3, 1891. Sumner was arrested again in late March for "subornation of perjury" when he attempted to bribe Cuthbert Saffery with $5,000 to go before Coroner Levy and identify the dead "Fred Evans" as George H. Edgar. As *The Sun* stated on April 1, 1891, "Mr. Sumner is one of the most unfortunate men in America, and he can trace all of his misfortune to his uncontrollable desire to collect dead Edgars." Most people believed that Sumner was involved in insurance fraud and held a policy on the life of a fictitious George H. Edgar.

A seemingly unrelated event occurred at the southern tip of Staten Island at the isolated village of Tottenville on the evening of March 11, 1891. The bound body of a brawny man was found floating in the water off Elliott's Dock. Covered with a sheet and lying on ice at the house of undertaker Isaac P. Bedell, the remains would be identified by Gustave S. Neu of 127 East Fifty-Eighth Street, Manhattan. By lantern light, Neu recognized the man as Carl Ruttinger, who had disappeared on February 2. Since Ruttinger's passport was found on the body, the identification was corroborated. Ruttinger and a male friend had rented a room from Neu on January 9 or 10. According to Neu, the partner was an Englishman, small in stature, with the accent of a Londoner. "His hands small and delicate, like those of a woman. His manner was also effeminate…a contrast to Ruttinger."[25] Quick and nervous, his name was William Wright. One acquaintance said of Wright, "His hands shook violently, and he wore a pained expression. No one who met Wright forgot him." Wright seemed to regard Ruttinger as the "head of their partnership. Apparently, he would do nothing without consulting Ruttinger first."[26] They had recently arrived from Europe, where Ruttinger worked in the lace-making business. Wright was a diamond setter. They were related by marriage. Neu said the two were like brothers and thought a great deal of each other. They never went out after dinner and instead spent every evening together in their room. He believed they were discouraged by their poor results in finding employment. But then Wright left for a Boston diamond-setting position on February 1. Ruttinger had applied for a number of jobs in the lace houses of New York City but had procured nothing. When found, the deceased had two Staten Island Rapid Transit Railroad coupons purchased on February 2 in his pocket.

With Ruttinger dead on a gurney, authorities wanted to know where Wright was. Ruttinger was married to Wright's sister Madge, who lived in London with another brother. Ruttinger and his wife originally lived in Italy but moved to Thaum, Germany, then to Dresden and, finally, to London. Wright was with them the whole time as Ruttinger's companion. Wright had no business; he was a gentleman of leisure. One acquaintance who knew Wright in Germany referred to him as a "dude," a man who did nothing but roll cigarettes and ride a bicycle. All the Wright offspring had inherited money from their father. The marriage of Carl and Madge began falling apart, and they were separated during summer 1890, with Mrs. Ruttinger leaving for England. Wright took Ruttinger's side in the couple's problems, and both men sailed for America onboard the *City of Chicago* on December 31, 1890—a new start for the New Year. They arrived on January 8. On January 22, Wright wrote home that he and Ruttinger were going to the western United States. If anything happened to him, he wanted his property to go to Mrs. Ruttinger and her two children by Carl. Meanwhile, it was discovered that Ruttinger had life insurance in the amount of $21,000, leading some to believe that it was "a graveyard insurance plot" geared to cash in on the insurance money. In other words, the body found floating off Tottenville was someone who resembled Carl Ruttinger and was dressed in

Left: A modern-day view of the Tottenville waterfront where Carl Ruttinger's body was discovered. *Photograph by Patricia M. Salmon, 2013.*

Right: William Wright. *From the* Auburn Bulletin, *March 27, 1891.*

his clothes. The charade was said to be completed by placing Ruttinger's passport in the coat's breast pocket.

Police took notice of the fact that Carl Ruttinger had been a Hercules while alive. They could not understand why he had not simply burst the weak twine that pinioned his arms when he was thrown in the water. For this reason, they questioned whether he was alive when the cord was tied. Another odd occurrence was that Ruttinger's body had no marks or cuts; there was no sign of a struggle. Even his shirt and tie were orderly, indicating that a tussle had not occurred. The handkerchief stuffed into his mouth bore the initials "W.W." Police could not fathom why he simply did not bite the fingers that thrust the cloth into his mouth. These two points left police thinking that the binding and the handkerchief were used to throw them off. No one could determine what had brought Ruttinger to that corner of Staten Island. Neu went so far as to declare that Ruttinger's placement in Staten Island was "remarkable."[27] When asked if he thought Wright murdered Ruttinger, Neu replied that it was impossible for someone as slight as Wright to bound and gag the bigger man against his will. In addition, the two train tickets in Ruttinger's pocket indicated he had a traveling companion. But where was Wright? Further confusion was realized when it was determined that Ruttinger had not drowned. He had suffocated because the handkerchief was so far down his throat that it had blocked both the nose and mouth air passages. Ruttinger's death was meant to look like a robbery/murder. He had no money on his person, and he was bound and gagged.

Everyone agreed that William Wright's silence on the discovery of his friend's dead body at Staten Island was suspicious. If he had not read about Ruttinger's death in the newspaper, why hadn't he at least written his friend to tell him how things were in Boston?

All of Ruttinger's personal effects, including clothing, jewelry and mail, were handed over to Richmond County District Attorney Fitzgerald and Police Chief Clarke. Fitzgerald got a break. Ruttinger's valise held negatives of the two men. Comparing the images with the man in the makeshift Tottenville morgue, Fitzgerald had no doubt that he was indeed Carl Ruttinger. Most important was the similarity between William Wright and the Astor House suicide, "Fred Evans." As such, photos of Wright were shown to morgue keeper White in Manhattan, who had held Evans's body before it was buried. He verified, without a doubt, that "Fred Evans" was William Wright, as did undertaker Duffy. When shown a photo of "Fred Evans" taken at the morgue, Gustave Neu verified that it was indeed Wright. The man had ended his own life at the Astor Hotel. District Attorney Fitzgerald went to check the clothing found in the dead man's room. On the boots, etched on the inside about an inch from the top, he found the letters "W.W." Guests often carved their initials into their boots when they were left in the hall for blacking. Another important find was made by Fitzgerald: the unique sand and red clay of Tottenville, Staten Island, still clung to the boots. A brand-new nickel was also found in Wright's pocket. The Staten Island Rapid Transit Railroad bought mass quantities of new nickels from the government to make exact change.

No matter what anyone said about Ruttinger's size or Wright's delicateness, Fitzgerald believed that Wright murdered Ruttinger. Perhaps Wright administered morphine to Ruttinger (at that time, morphine would leave no detectable trace in the body), which knocked him out, and then killed him by some unknown means on February 2. Then, sometime during the following three hours, Wright went to the Astor House and, whether due to remorse or some other cause, sliced his own throat. The district attorney could not suggest a motive.

Even though he had been positively identified, theories still abounded about the identity of the Tottenville body. He was said to be Charles Schneider, first mate of the ship *Momsen*. But when a cousin by marriage

Left: Richmond County District Attorney Thomas Fitzgerald worked tirelessly to identify both William Wright and Carl Ruttinger. *From* A Memorial History of Staten Island, *1898.*

Below: Receiving and removing dead bodies at the New York City morgue. *From* Treat's Illustrated New York: Brooklyn and Surroundings, *1874.*

Opposite: Corpses at the New York City morgue awaiting identification. *From* Treat's Illustrated New York: Brooklyn and Surroundings, *1874.*

examined the body, he was certain that it was not Schneider, as the deceased lacked a blue-and-red anchor tattoo on his left arm.

Landlord Neu also reported receiving an odd letter from Rochester, New Hampshire native John Campbell, who claimed that a stranger looking very much like the description of "Fred Evans" arrived in that town on February 25. The community was suspicious, as the man had become very anxious when someone walked into his boardinghouse room and discovered him picking through three well-filled wallets. Equally strange was his arrival without baggage and the unusual number of keys he carried on his person. The stranger also had a skillful manner of tying children's hands behind their back, which reminded the writer of Ruttinger's bound hands. The man left the boardinghouse on March 13 without paying his bill. He tried to rent a room ten miles away, but when he was unable to pay up front, he was sent away. The writer had no doubt the man was running from justice.

On March 24, a Mrs. Ploech of 123rd Street in Manhattan claimed the Astor House victim was Edward C. Smith, a clerk in Macy's china department. When contacted, Mr. Smith fervently denied that the dead body was his. Interestingly, Mrs. Ploech later refuted making the statement about Edward C. Smith. She said it was Perrin Sumner who said it was

James H. Edgar using the Smith alias and that Sumner offered her money to say that the body was Edgar alias Smith. Another report had Wright hanging by the neck in a Massachusetts farmer's barn.

Fred Evans, better known as William Wright, was dug out of the frozen black mud of Potter's Field at Hart's Island on March 18, 1891. There was no marker; it was simply labeled on a map as Coffin 85 in Plot 169. Two paupers were given five dollars each and the use of New York City pickaxes to get the plain pine box out of the muck. Water poured out of a hole in the box as it was lifted out. When the box was opened, the body was embalmed in mud. Former landlord Gustave Neu was there, and he positively identified the body as that of Wright. District Attorney Fitzgerald regarded the identification as certain and complete. By this time, specific facts on Wright's life had been revealed. Apprenticed to a diamond cutter, he could not stay with the trade, so he was released from the indenture. He then took money inherited from his father's death and went to live with Ruttinger and his wife in Germany, where he invested the money in Ruttinger's business. But the venture failed, and Wright's money was not recovered. After Ruttinger and Wright relocated to New York, letters sent home prior to January 22, 1891, expressed their disappointment at having little success in the New World. They were not heard from again.

Undertaker Bedell prepared Carl Ruttinger's body for burial by covering it with a black shroud and laying it in a black cloth casket. In the presence of a large number of village residents, Carl Ruttinger was buried at the Bethel Methodist Episcopal Church Cemetery in Tottenville on March 17 1891, as the church bell tolled the dead man's age. He was buried far from his home with the permission of his wife and family. Obviously, they were done with the man. None attended the service except District Attorney Fitzgerald. With Reverend Mr. Wigg and the Reverend Mr. Robinson co-officiating, Ruttinger was buried under the Tottenville sand next to the grave of Chaplain John L. Lenhart, who had been killed during the Civil War.

As the investigation unfolded, the people of Staten Island were displeased at the money Fitzgerald had spent on the Ruttinger/Wright affair. There was a call for shutting down the inquiry. After all, neither man was a Staten Island resident. They weren't even citizens of the United States.

Some still refused to believe the Astor House suicide was William Wright, but on April 2, 1891, the inquest jury announced that the suicide victim was William Wright and that Perrin Sumner's audacious attempt to identify the body as an Edgar was an effort to pervert justice.

Above: Terracotta sign at the Bethel Methodist Episcopal Church, where Carl Ruttinger's burial occurred. *Photograph by Patricia M. Salmon, 2013.*

Left: The Bethel Methodist Episcopal Church. *Photograph by Patricia M. Salmon, 2013.*

On April 3, 1891, the remains of William Wright were again buried—this time at Greenwood Cemetery in Brooklyn, as per the Wright family's attorney. Meanwhile, Perrin Sumner remained locked up in the Tombs prison in Manhattan—but not for long. Sumner was soon released without any conviction on the matter.

At the inquest, Dr. Walser reported that neither alcohol nor mineral poisoning was found in Ruttinger's stomach, just some German herring salad and beets. This nullified the theory that the big man was drunk and overtaken by an assailant. Furthermore, Walser believed the bonds had been tied after Ruttinger was unconscious or dead, as there were no marks on the flesh from the cords. Dr. Caleb Lyons of Rossville testified that Ruttinger's death was a case of suicide to simulate murder. It was his belief that the act was carefully planned—that Wright assisted Ruttinger by binding him and

After identification, the remains of William Wright were permanently interred at Greenwood Cemetery in Brooklyn. *From* Treat's Illustrated New York: Brooklyn and Surroundings, *1874.*

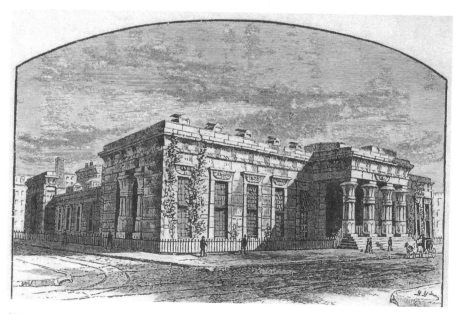

Charlatan Perrin Summer was locked up at the Tombs prison in Manhattan. *From* New York Illustrated, *1891.*

then stuffing the handkerchief into his mouth. Ruttinger then "walked out into the water, where he fell, overcome by the gagging, into the soft mud where his body was found." If it had been a murder, there was no doubt in Lyon's mind that owing to Ruttinger's size and build he could easily have released himself from the twine and simple knots utilized. He declared it was "self-murder committed with the aid of a second party." Even so, the inquest jury ruled that Ruttinger's death was "at the hands of some person or persons unknown and that the cause of death was suffocation by the cramming of a handkerchief down his throat."[28]

The handkerchief stuffed into Ruttinger's mouth was soon identified as belonging to William Wright. Wright's family sent two from England. When compared with the one in police custody, it was said that the details, including the cloth and the size and style of type, were identical, as were the initials: "W.W."

Could the slight Wright have murdered Ruttinger, a man who was physically described as athletic and robust? Was Ruttinger's death a suicide resulting from disappointed ambition, an ill-spent life and marital unhappiness? Was it an insurance hoax? Ruttinger no doubt knew the insurance would not be paid on a suicide, so was it an elaborate attempt to make his death appear as a murder? Had a double been used? Was Ruttinger still alive to share the insurance money? Why was Ruttinger put out by his wife? Why was Wright determined to kill himself after he assisted Ruttinger with his suicide in Tottenville? Was Ruttinger killed for the money he supposedly had when he arrived from Europe? Early reports said he was well off, but his activities and commentary about employment indicated otherwise.

For all the sensational newspaper headlines featuring Ruttinger and Wright, there was one small postscript a year later. On page nine of the *New York Herald* of February 16, 1892, the title read simply "Ruttinger's Policy Paid." Mrs. Therese Ruttinger of Stuttgart, Germany, Carl Ruttinger's mother, received a $32,000 payment from the Equitable Life Assurance Society. The company stated there was no proof of suicide from the police, so it paid the claim.

Chapter 5

THE STATEN ISLAND TERROR

They were on a spree. Drunk and searching for more drink, they barreled up to the New York Avenue saloon of Frederick Mahlfeld in Clifton as the barkeep's wife was locking up. It was after midnight on March 18, 1894, so it was a Sunday, and selling alcohol was against the law. Even so, the three toughs pounded on the tavern door demanding admittance. With that, twenty-four-year-old Martin McNamara came to Mrs. Mahlfeld's aid to secure and lock the door. The varmints went away but soon returned with a log to serve as a battering ram. They splintered the door and attacked. Mr. Mahlfeld quickly fled, so they turned their attention on McNamara. The fight spilled into the street, and a crowd gathered, causing the combatants to separate. This allowed McNamara to retreat to Bay View Avenue, but the ruthless brutes regrouped, followed McNamara, knocked him to the ground and savagely kicked him. McNamara was finally assisted by Thomas O'Neill, who helped him escape. Even so, the thugs found McNamara again and beat him into insensibility. Never regaining consciousness, he died at his Second Street home in Clifton. It was the opinion of Dr. T.J. Thompson that McNamara had died from a fracture at the base of the skull. "Old Mrs. McNamara was almost wild at the death of her son. She knelt at the coffin all afternoon and could not be induced to leave it."[29] For his part, saloonkeeper Frederick Mahlfeld opened for business as usual.

Three potential murderers—Harry Keeley, Gustave Schiedmantel and Philip Hagelstein—were arrested. All had bad reputations, with Keeley having been collared for involvement in the local murder of Harry Clark a

Usually peaceful, Clifton was a village of simple homes and estates such as this one, owned by A.L. King. *From* History of Richmond County, Staten Island, *1887.*

Martin McNamara and saloonkeeper Frederick Mahlfeld alongside his Clifton establishment. *From* The World, *March 19, 1894.*

few years earlier. On the other hand, Martin McNamara had an excellent character. He took care of his widowed mother and worked diligently for the Staten Island Rapid Transit Railroad.

Interestingly, Harry Keeley was the brother of a newly elected town clerk, James D. Keeley. A carpenter by trade, Keeley also made a career of being arrested for drunkenness and fighting. Schiedmantel was a machinist's apprentice, while Hagelstein was a sailor.

Harry Keeley pleaded guilty to manslaughter in the second degree for the death of Martin McNamara on Halloween Day 1894. On November 2, 1894, he was removed to begin his sentence at Sing Sing Prison. Keeley received only three years and two months for his part in McNamara's slaying. Schiedmantel pleaded guilty to assault in the third degree. Hagelstein was discharged due to lack of evidence but was dead only two years later. While onboard the steamer *Acapulco* at Panama, he died at the age of twenty-two on September 27, 1896.

Upon release, Harry Keeley returned to Staten Island and his old habits. During late February 1898, an intoxicated Harry and his brothers, William and John, had a vicious quarrel in their home. It spilled into the street, with Harry firing three pistol shots at his brothers. The brothers were not hit, but a passerby, Perry Stobell, took a bullet to the groin. While the wound was not life threatening, it was extremely painful. Keeley was brought before Judge Marsh and arraigned for assault with intent to kill. (By the time he was thirty, Harry Keeley had spent half his life in jail for one crime or another.)

On June 28, 1903, Harry Keeley pumped three bullets into Policeman James McGrath at Broad Street in Stapleton. It began the day before. With a pistol and 134 cartridges of ammunition, Keeley went from saloon to saloon boasting that he would kill a policeman and gladly go to the electric chair. By the time he was released from Sing Sing for McNamara's murder, Keeley had developed a keen hatred for police and his fellow man. Over the years, his sanity was questioned and he was even committed to ninety days of psychiatric observation at Manhattan Hospital early in 1903 for a savage fight he instigated. For some reason, Keeley was back on the street thirty days later.

As he went from saloon to saloon, Keeley proudly displayed his pistol and made wild threats, which were reported to Officer James McGrath. The officer located Keeley at the corner of Broad and Centre Streets and ordered him to go home. Keeley refused, so McGrath again ordered him to go home. With that, Keeley pulled out the pistol and fired five shots. The first lodged above McGrath's heart. The second went into his right shoulder,

Stapleton was better known for its industry, shops and tradesmen until Harry Keeley shot Officer James McGrath. *From* An Illustrated Sketchbook of Staten Island, *1886.*

while the third ripped the fingers of his right hand. Two bullets went wild—much like Harry Keeley. Watching from a distance was John Fritz. For this reason, he, too, was shot. When Keeley was finally subdued, it took four men to hold him still at the police station. Every pocket on Keeley was filled with bullets. Surprisingly, McGrath survived the attack. Keeley was arraigned on July 16, 1903, and was indicted for assault in the first degree. A commission was finally established to determine Harry Keeley's sanity, and of course he was determined to be insane. The finding was announced on October 16, 1903, as was his placement in the Dannemora Asylum in upstate New York.

During December 1919, doctors called for Keeley's release from Matteawan State Hospital for the Criminally Insane. After sixteen years, all that was needed was the consent of the Richmond County district attorney. Dr. R.F.C. Keib and his assistant, Dr. Moore, agreed that Harry was a reasonably safe risk to be allowed out. Having inherited part of an estate during his hospitalization, Harry was planning to move closer to relatives in the western United States in order to start over at the age of forty-five.

Chapter 6
REVENGE RENEWS OUR HAPPY LOVE IN HEAVEN FOREVER

It was 4:00 a.m. on January 26, 1907. Dr. Charles W. Townsend, one of Staten Island's most respected physicians and surgeons, was asleep in his bed at 5 Westervelt Avenue, New Brighton. Exhausted from seventy-five medical calls the previous day, when the phone next to the doctor's bed rang, it barely woke him. As he slightly opened his eyes, a man with a lit match in one hand and a revolver in the other stood before him. With the revolver pointed at the doctor, the invader, whose face was wrapped in a handkerchief, said, "Get up you," to which Dr. Townsend responded, "I will." Before he could move, the intruder shot Townsend in the abdomen. With that, Mrs. Townsend screamed and called the trespasser a coward for shooting an unarmed man. She ordered him to put down his weapon. Instead, he fled, but before he reached the door, he turned and fired another bullet into the doctor's thigh. Mrs. Townsend ran to the bedroom window and screamed into the yard. This brought neighbor Lawrence Crabtree running, while the Townsend nurse, Mary Flint, attempted to call police from the downstairs phone. She discovered the line cut, but another line was intact, so the call was made.

Police found Mrs. Townsend, a physician herself, dressing her husband's wounds. She had already administered a dose of morphine. Conscious, Dr. Townsend was placed in an ambulance that headed for the S.R. Smith Infirmary. It was said by some that he stated, "I won't name the one who did it. It is better that one should die than two." But his chauffeur, Joseph Hayes, told police that Townsend said, "It was Silverman or someone who resembled him."[30]

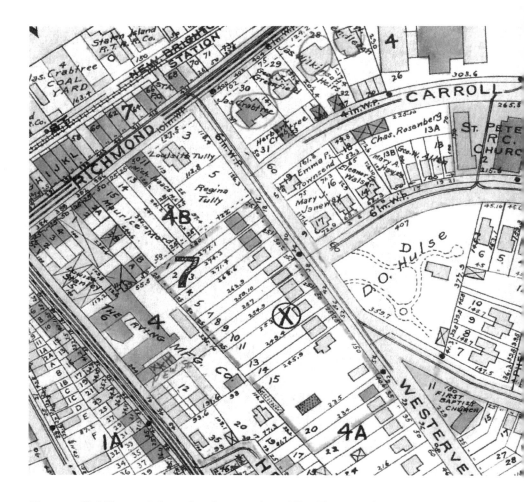

Coroner Cahill stated that when he questioned Dr. Townsend, he was told that the doctor had no idea who fired the shots, that the shooter only resembled Silverman. Even so, Moses Silverman was taken into custody and brought before Dr. Townsend as he lay dying in the hospital. Staring at Silverman, Townsend would say only that he looked something like the shooter. Later, Silverman's brother-in-law Isaac Schneider was also taken into custody. Police said he resembled the description given by both Dr. and Mrs. Townsend more so than Silverman. Both men denied any responsibility, saying that they had been at home when the shooting occurred. Inspector Schmittberger did not take much stock in the arrests since neither man had a grudge against the good doctor. Schneider even stated, "This is a foolish thing. We love Dr. Townsend. Two years ago, when my wife was sick for a week, Dr. Townsend attended her.

Above: Dr. Charles Wilmot Townsend had the misfortune of admitting Mamie Bell to the Smith Infirmary in 1906. *From* A Memorial History of Staten Island, *1898.*

Left: Location of the Dr. and Mrs. Charles W. Townsend home on Westervelt Avenue in New Brighton. *From* E. Robinson Atlas of Richmond County, *1907.*

I am a poor man. Dr. Townsend knew this, and when I went to pay the bill, he tore it up."[31]

When he arrived at the hospital, Dr. Townsend informed the staff that he had no chance of survival. The first bullet had sliced his intestine six times and stopped at his spine. The second had gone through his leg and into the bed. The infirmary reported that Dr. Townsend was in critical condition. There was little hope for recovery.

Schmittberger soon realized that robbery had not been the motive, as $200 in a purse and assorted diamonds were casually lying on the main bedroom bureau. Dr. Townsend's .32 caliber gun was fully loaded, so that ruled out Mrs. Townsend as the shooter—besides, it was later found that the bullets were from a .36 caliber revolver. Police soon discovered that the eldest Townsend child, Louisa, was awake when the murderer turned on the hallway light before entering her parent's bedroom. Since a downstairs dining room window was kept open, as Dr. Townsend was a great believer in fresh air, it was not difficult for the intruder to gain access to the house. Mrs. Townsend was so overcome with shock that her account of the crime was inconsistent. One thing that police and the Townsend family agreed upon was that revenge in response to a supposed neglect on the part of Dr. Townsend's medical care was probably the prime motive, even though all agreed that he was known for the devoted care that he gave to all. Also known for his generosity, the doctor often provided free medical services for the poor. His last known call was to a neighbor. Mrs. Crabtree had fallen on the ice and sprained her wrist. The doctor came right over and bandaged it, after which he chatted amicably with the ladies of the house. All noted that he was in a happy state of mind. Ironically, Townsend told one neighbor he hadn't an enemy in the world.

Richmond County District Attorney John Kenney was horrified at the police investigation. Aghast that they had taken the Sunday after the murder off, he called the police work deplorable. Kenney declared that a reporter or a citizen would discover the identity of the shooter before the police department.

The Townsend family soon reported that the doctor vehemently denied knowing the identity of the shooter. Stories about Dr. Townsend having amorous adventures with women resulting in a jealous husband or beau shooting him began to circulate. These rumors were renounced by the family as being common for successful physicians. They asserted no such motive existed. Eyebrows were raised when it came to light that Mrs. Townsend had separated from her husband for a few weeks several years previous. After friends brought about a reconciliation, she moved back into their Westervelt Avenue family home. At the time, she stated it was for the sake of the children.

The murder was shrouded in mystery. Many were comparing it to the odd death of Charles Spier, a friend of Dr. Townsend who lived not far away at 7 Tompkins Avenue. Ruled a suicide, numerous individuals, including some on the police force, believed it was murder. Perhaps there was a connection to the slaying of Dr. Townsend?

With his wife and other family members by his side, Dr. Charles Wilmot Townsend died in the S.R. Smith Infirmary at 1:00 a.m. on January 27, 1907. Townsend was a graduate, third in a class of two hundred, of the College of Physicians and Surgeons. He was also an alumnus of the School of Mines of Columbia University, and at the time of his death, he was vice-president of the Richmond County Medical Society. His wife, Emma Townsend, was the daughter of Dr. Theodore Walser and sister of Dr. William Walser. While in the hospital, Townsend was administered to by his brother-in-law and by Dr. William Bryan (fiancé of Mary Tobin, who also died mysteriously).

On the same day that Dr. Townsend died, Detectives O'Connor and Galvin of the Mulberry Street Police Station and a squad of officers surrounded the 648 Hart Street residence of John Bell. Refused admittance to the Williamsburg, Brooklyn home by John's father, Samuel Bell, authorities forced their way in to search for John. They hunted from attic to cellar and finally came upon a little man in a darkened third-floor room. Crouched in a corner, he was no more than five feet tall with "the face of an old man and the body of a child."[32] Police found a concealed silk handkerchief on Bell's person. It closely resembled the one covering the assassin's face as described by Mrs. Townsend. When brought into the police station, the spectators laughed that such a puny man would have the nerve to confront a man of Dr. Townsend's physique. While declaring that he did not shoot Townsend, Bell did acknowledge the doctor "was no friend of his." As he was led out of the station for transport to the Tombs Prison, Bell called out to the gathered crowd, "You needn't worry about me—I have nothing to be afraid of."[33]

Bell was arrested because of the many virulent threats he voiced against Dr. Townsend—threats that had eventually come to the ears of Policeman Krause of the Hamburg Avenue station in Brooklyn. Bell's stepmother, Alice, later told police that John had actually admitted killing the doctor the day of the shooting! (Mrs. Bell later denied making this statement.) Officer Krause also learned that Bell had been missing the entire night of the murder and had not returned to the Hart Street home until after 8:00 a.m.

According to police, while living at 72 Montgomery Street in Tompkinsville, Staten Island, John Bell went to the home of Dr. Charles W. Townsend on January 25, 1906. His wife, Mamie, was ill again. After a long delay, the doctor had her admitted to the S.R. Smith Infirmary, but at 4:00 a.m. the following morning, Mamie Bell died. Bell became obsessed with Mamie's death and ceaselessly blamed Dr. Townsend, whom he swore to kill one day. When his revenge was realized, Bell vowed he would take his own life on Mamie's grave at Cypress Hills Cemetery. Bell went so far as to have the phrase "Revenge renews our happy love in heaven forever"[34] engraved on Mamie's tombstone during January 1907. In addition, police found witnesses who had seen John Bell on Staten Island days before the shooting. Law enforcement attempted to have Mrs. Townsend identify the prisoner at the Tombs, but she declined, stating that she was too distraught and ill. When the prisoner was brought to the home of District Attorney John Kenney for Mrs. Townsend to identify, she was still in such a state and refused to look at him.

John Bell met Mamie Meighan when he was a streetcar conductor. Owing to his emaciated body, he was often the subject of ridicule. Most women refused to have anything to do with him. But Mamie didn't make fun of his small stature, and as such, Bell worshiped her and treated her like a doll. "All the starved emotion within his dwarfed body he poured out on Mamie."[35]

Because her parents refused to consent to their marriage, they eloped and settled on Staten Island.

According to hospital records, Mamie died from Bright's disease and convulsions. In addition, Mamie was pregnant, and when she died, the infant was born—but it died, too. John Bell was devastated. Ironically, Townsend had little to do with her hospital care aside from her admittance. She was under the care of another physician.

After Mamie's death, Bell left Staten Island a very distraught man. Wandering to New England and then to San Francisco, he encountered the great earthquake of April 18, 1906. When he returned east, he worked as a streetcar conductor in the Bronx. On his days off, he went to Cypress Hill Cemetery. Sporadically, he stayed with his father and stepmother in Brooklyn. The rest of the time, he simply disappeared. As the anniversary of his wife's death got closer, he became sullen and moody and often muttered, "That doctor might have saved Mamie. He shouldn't have let her die." During his blacker moments, he said, "Mamie shouldn't lie alone."[36] Then, for no reason, a strange cheerfulness descended upon Bell.

On the day of the murder, John Bell maintained that he had gone to the Thalia Theatre in the Bowery to see *A Marked Woman*. Afterward, claiming that "he did the Bowery," meaning he went from gin joint to gin joint for the remainder of the night, he arrived home after 8:00 a.m. District Attorney John Kenney told Bell that if he provided him with an alibi, he would personally see that it was thoroughly investigated, and that if it were true, he would quickly release Bell. But Bell refused to say a word other than that he had attended the theater and visited the saloons afterward.

Evidence against Bell mounted. Police recovered seven letters written by the accused to family members. In one to his brother Howard, he requested that the appropriate inscription be placed on his headstone and that he make sure the ring was on his finger, the slippers on his feet and the picture on his breast. He asked Howard to "pray that I might be justified in my act and that I meet her [Mamie] in Heaven and that God be merciful."[37]

Police spoke to Maurice Mord, a storeowner on Shore Road in New Brighton not far from the Townsend home. Mord told police that a "little man" had come into his store at about 4:00 p.m. on the day of Townsend's murder. He left but returned at approximately 6:00 p.m. Appearing very nervous, he purchased a handkerchief. When shown Bell's photo, Mord immediately verified that he was the man. Later that night, trolley worker John Lee saw a small man in a black raincoat on the trolley trestle by the Staten Island

Ferry terminal. He took note of the trespasser, as walking in the area was forbidden. When police searched John Bell's room, they found a black raincoat, and they noted that the terminal was less than a ten-minute run from the Townsend house. Police also discovered that Bell owned two revolvers that were not located during the first search of his residence. His stepbrother Samuel later admitted removing the guns to a friend's house. They were eventually recovered and found freshly oiled and filled with bullets.

In describing John Bell, District Attorney Kenney called him "a little cat of a man with all of a cat's caution and cunning." Owing to his size and skill, the "slight and wiry" Bell had made his way through the Townsend house with little notice.

District Attorney John Kenney vowed that he would thoroughly investigate any alibi provided by John Bell. *From* A Memorial History of Staten Island, *1898.*

He had watched the sleeping doctor for some time and had even gone to the end of the hall and peered into one of the bedrooms, where an elderly woman lay sleeping. Relatives later said he contemplated whether he should proceed with the murder since the doctor had people who depended on him but that he then remembered Mamie and said to himself, "I'll avenge Mamie. This man killed her."[38] But again, looking in another room, he saw two little girls sleeping, and for a brief moment, he reconsidered shooting Townsend. Again, his heart hardened so he entered the physician's bedroom and struck the match.

After the shooting, Bell fled from the house and ran to the ferry terminal at Saint George. As he approached the building, he slowed his gait and acted as naturally as possible. Even so, a policeman approached and asked what he was doing about at that hour. Bell responded that he worked for a newspaper and had irregular hours. By 8:30 a.m., he was at his brother-in-law's saloon on Rodney Street in Brooklyn. He asked if he had heard about the Townsend shooting, to which the brother-in-law said no. Bell responded, "I guess it's about up with me now." He then gave the barkeeper $2.50 to buy the boys a keg of beer on Thursday, as "he himself would be out of the world by then."[39]

Bell's family rallied around him, with his father being the first to say that it was not unusual for his son to stay out all night, as had happened the night Townsend was murdered. In addition, Samuel Bell said that he never overheard his son making threats against the doctor, adding, "My boy wouldn't harm a cat. Why, he was even afraid of a firecracker."[40]

Fearing incarceration if they continued to hide the true story of John Bell's descent into madness and killing, the family finally cracked and told all. Inspector Schmittberger believed that John Bell was insane from cigarette smoking. In a thirteen-hour period, Bell reportedly smoked four packs of cigarettes and three cigars. Schmittberger maintained that Bell's "fingers are stained with nicotine, as is the case with all 'fiends.'"[41] One account actually had Bell smoking ten packs of cigarettes per day.

On January 29, Moses Silverman was released. Indignant over his unnecessary incarceration, he swore a lawsuit against the police for false arrest. That same afternoon, Dr. Townsend was finally laid to rest after a funeral at his home. Originally, the service was to be held at St. John's Church in Clifton, but owing to the number of mourners, it was decided that his house was a better location. Burial was at Moravian Cemetery in New Dorp.

Bell was finally brought before Mrs. Townsend for identification on February 5, with the result that she could not swear he was the man who had shot her husband. The prosecutor even put a handkerchief over Bell's face and a derby hat on his head, two items the killer had worn the night of the murder. Even after being accessorized, Mrs. Townsend was unsure.

On May 20, 1907, with Judge George B. Abbott presiding, John Bell went on trial at the Richmond County Courthouse. Out of forty potential jurors, eight were chosen that first day. Many were excused because they would not convict a man on circumstantial evidence. On May 22, commotion heralded in the courtroom's proceeding when John Bell switched lawyers. Dissatisfied with the work of Frederick Milligan, he hired attorney Edward O'Reilly of Brooklyn. No sooner had the change been executed when Claude Holterman, a daily spectator at the trial, staggered and fell to the ground. Local physician Dr. Devlin arrived on the scene to pronounce Holterman dead of heart failure. Even so, the trial continued.

William Coar, Bell's brother-in-law, proved to be a most unwilling witness. Verbal testimony was not dragged out until his previously signed statement came before the court. He finally acknowledged that Bell had come to his tavern the morning after the murder and stated, "I've just killed the doctor." When Coar asked why, Bell replied, "Well, I got revenge."[42] John's Bell's stepmother then took the stand. She acknowledged hearing

Saint John's Church in Clifton. Originally selected for the site of the Townsend funeral, it was instead performed at his home. *From* A Memorial History of Staten Island, *1898.*

Bell say he took revenge on a doctor but stated that he did not mention the doctor by name.

Then Mrs. Townsend dramatically recounted the murderous events of the morning of January 26, but again, she could not verify that John Bell was the murderer. She would say only that Bell resembled the intruder. District Attorney Kenney stunned the courtroom the following day when he produced a photograph showing Mamie Bell's headstone with the prominent epitaph "Revenge renews our happy love in heaven forever." When he saw the photo, Bell "quailed for the first time since the trial began" and his "face became ashen."[43] Damaging testimony was further inflicted by Howard Bell as he described John's visit the night after the murder. Calling his half brother outside, he told him he had shot a Staten Island doctor.

The one and only witness called by the defense was John Bell. When cross-examination was complete, Bell passionately jumped up and shouted his innocence. In a rambling statement, he claimed poverty had brought him into court. Bell believed money would have produced witnesses to verify his whereabouts during the time of the killing. Furthermore, he asserted that he shouldn't be executed on circumstantial evidence. Pointing at his face, he asked the jury, "Do I look to you like a murderer?" He implored them to look at his hands and said, "Do you think they held the gun that killed Dr. Townsend?"[44] Most people agreed. Why hadn't Bell's lawyer simply attempted to prove he was insane?

After a deliberation of two hours and fifty-nine minutes on May 23, 1907, the jury found John Bell guilty of murdering Dr. Charles Wilmot Townsend. Judge Abbott quickly pronounced the penalty as death by electric chair. Bell remained calm, but his stepmother let out a piercing shriek and fainted to the ground, while his sister also fell unconscious by her side. Both women were revived by Dr. Devlin and were led weeping from the courtroom. Stating that he had been handed a lemon, Bell was calmly escorted from the court back to the Richmond Jail, where he would await transfer to the death house at Sing Sing for a July 1 execution. As he was removed, the killer swore there was no possibility of execution.

By January 31, the practice of Dr. Charles Wilmot Townsend was on the market. His home, medical instruments, library, stable, horses, carriage and automobile were advertised, with the ad stressing that the practice brought in $12,000 to $15,000 annually. Lively bidding characterized the sale. Smith Infirmary operating surgeon Dr. A.H. Thomas of Clifton successfully bought the house for $16,000. With the property sold, Mrs. Townsend planned to live in the Saint Mark's Avenue home of her sister, Mrs. Janeway.

For his fine work in clearing up the Townsend murder, Inspector Schmittberger was rewarded with a promotion to commander of the Manhattan Traffic Squad. The police commissioner actually transferred or promoted three other top-ranking officers to move Schmittberger, who was initially transferred to Staten Island, owing to a complaint made against him by a deputy police commissioner. (An assignment in Staten Island was more or less a punishment for New York City police. The *New York Tribune* of February 6, 1907, even heralded the announcement with the headline "Schmittberger Back," as if he was previously stationed in a foreign country.)

Later that year, Bell's attorney filed a notice of appeal, and the convict received a stay of execution. Unbelievably, by the standards of that time, the Court of Appeals still had not heard the case by July 1910. While incarcerated at Sing Sing, Bell began exhibiting signs of insanity, so a commission was formed by then-governor Charles Hughes to determine his mental stability. As such, he was deemed insane and transferred to Dannemora State Hospital for the Criminally Insane. He died there at the age of sixty-two on January 19, 1941.

By the time of her death on September 13, 1916, Emma Townsend had returned to her medical training and was referred to as Dr. Townsend—Dr. Emma Albertina Walser Townsend, to be exact. In addition, she was a member of the Staten Island Board of Education, president of the Staten Island Women's Club and an active member of the Brighton Heights

Reformed Church. Her obituary noted that she was the first female interne in a New York hospital and the first interne at the New York Babies Hospital.

Acknowledging the centennial anniversary of the murder of Dr. Charles Wilmot Townsend, his great-grandson placed an article in an online newspaper. Scott Herhold's focus was not only to memorialize the doctor but also to recognize the effect this murder had on one particular family member. Fourteen-year-old Louise Townsend was the lone occupant of the house awake while John Bell paced back and forth in the hallway debating whether he should kill Dr. Townsend. She was cognizant of his final entrance into her parent's bedroom and pulling the trigger. She was so frightened that the invader would shoot her that she stayed in her bed, as silent and still as could be.

Like many of her relatives, Louise chose the medical profession and became a doctor. Her great nephew Scott and his wife visited the ninety-year-old "crusty, white haired" lifetime smoker in 1983. One of her first questions to them was, "Do you want a bourbon?" "She brought it in shakily on a silver tray," said Herhold. Scott was advised not to mention the murder, but his curiosity got the best of him, and he casually asked about the portrait of the handsome gentleman over the fireplace. It was Dr. Charles Wilmot Townsend. The elderly woman replied that it was her father. "Then she broke into tears, sobbing so much that our interview was over." Herhold felt like a "cad" but learned a lesson from the episode: "Time does not heal all wounds. I've always given Louise the benefit of the doubt because she was only 14 when her father died. But she gave me the feeling that she never forgave herself."[45]

Chapter 7
THREE BULLETS FOR THE BOOTLEGGER

As daylight came to South Beach, Staten Island, on August 21, 1920, a curious night watchman found the slain, slumped body of Frederick Eckert in an abandoned Packard touring car. Three bullets were lodged in his brain. Thus began one of the most bizarre chapters in Staten Island's crime history.

Alternately known as Robert Hayes, Robert Eckert, R.F. Eckert, Frederick Eckert and Robert Eckett (it would finally be determined that the real name of the corpse was Frederick Eckert), he had been released from the notorious Tombs Prison just one week previous. A criminal, he was well known to both federal agents and local police as a bootlegger. It was the era of Prohibition—that time in American history when it was illegal to manufacture, sell or transport alcoholic beverages. Enforcement of the law had gone into effect only a few months before on January 17, 1920. Prohibition made it rewarding for criminals to make fast bucks that were quite illegal, since the drinking public thirsted for alcohol and most believed outlawing alcohol was simply ridiculous. Men like Frederick Eckert were only too willing to risk time behind bars to satisfy the citizenry as well as their own wallets. But Frederick Eckert paid the ultimate price.

Early reports said he was a Prohibition enforcement agent, a myth that was soon debunked. It was also rumored that he was a "stool pigeon" who provided federal authorities with information on the sale of contraband liquor to the speakeasies and saloonkeepers of South Beach. It was firmly believed by the authorities that this led to his murder.

Illegal transports of liquor were often delivered at Midland and South Beaches during Prohibition. Postcard of Midland Beach, circa 1907. *Courtesy of Cheryl Criaris-Bontales.*

Twenty-nine-year-old Frederick Eckert's arrests involved everything from stealing cars to transporting stolen alcohol. The summer of 1920 had been a busy one for Eckert. Held for possessing pilfered liquor near Hopatcong, New Jersey, Eckert had kicked out the side of a jail while the sheriff went to lunch with Newark agents who were picking Eckert up because he was out on bail for a stolen-car charge when the Hopatcong arrest occurred.

During his escapades, Eckert occasionally stayed at Maloney's Manhattan Hotel at South Beach. Right on the beach, it was a known haunt for 1920s bootleggers, a place where swift boats secretly dropped off crates of illegal hooch. Eckert's permanent residence was in Orange, New Jersey. Known to don a badge and pose as a Prohibition agent when necessary, many remembered the night he held up three men at Maloney's. Clearly, Robert Eckert was "all over the place" when it came to crime.

Eckert's dead body was found outside the Perry and Austen paint factory on Old Town Road (now Olympia Boulevard) in South Beach. The vehicle was owned by Charles Kane of 233 Jewett Avenue, who had reported it stolen at 2:00 a.m. the morning Eckert was killed. Between 3:00 a.m. and 4:00 a.m., the factory's night watchman heard voices outside the building. When his dog started barking, he went out to investigate and found two men walking away from the touring car. The men claimed, "We've had some hard luck. Our car is stuck, and we're looking for the way to the beach."[46]

A more observant day watchman became curious about the car after his mongrel dog Nellie repeatedly whined at the abandoned car. William Mitchell stepped up to the car's running board and saw Eckert dead in the

Location of Frederick Eckert's murder outside the Perry and Austen paint factory at South Beach. *From the* Bromley Atlas of Richmond County, *1917.*

front seat. "His head was sunk between his knees, and he leaned with the tilt of the machine against the door. His straw hat lay at his feet in a puddle of blood."[47] It was Assistant Medical Examiner Dr. George P. Mord who found the three bullet wounds in the head. No other trauma was observed. The bullets had been fired at close range. There was no evidence of a struggle. Eckert was dapperly dressed in a neat blue serge suit, a silk shirt and socks and low, tan shoes. He had twenty-eight dollars, a gold watch and chain, a signet ring and cufflinks that bore the initials "R.F.E."

The first watchman provided a good description of the men. They were believed to be members of a mob operating on Staten Island. For some reason, police refused to provide the men's description to newspapers or the public. They theorized that Eckert had been killed by "dry agents," federal men responsible for enforcing the Prohibition laws who were themselves illegally reselling confiscated liquor. Supposedly, these agents had killed Eckert so that he could not rat them out. It was believed the federal agents had induced a saloonkeeper to put up bail for Eckert's release from the Tombs. Quite simply, the agents were pitting bootleggers against each other.

They would pinch cargo from one set and resell it to a friendly mob. Federal Supervising Prohibition Agent James Shevlin insisted the accused officials were law abiding.

The biggest whiskey hold-up to date occurred on August 3, 1920, and Frederick Eckert was there. "A caravan of motor trucks, en route at night with stores of whiskey, was held up in quick succession and their contents swiftly transshipped to other trucks. The plunder of this night was said to be more than $40,000." Eckert, police said, had numerous meetings with Prohibition agents. Staten Island District Attorney Joseph F. Maloy predicted "sensational developments" in the case, with "at least one well-known Federal employee"[48] connected to the murder.

Staten Island was fast becoming known as "Little Cuba," owing to the continuous arrival and storage of contraband liquor. Robbed shipments, Eckert's murder, and investigations into the possible federal agent involvement in trafficking stolen spirits was adding to the island's reputation. Staten Island was so saturated with illicit booze it was said to be "dripping wet!"

Authorities stated that no one was "more bold and reckless in daring arrest and more impudent in boasting that he possessed immunity from prosecution"[49] than Eckert. Clues and suspects were supplied by Eckert's widow, Florence. Arriving at the Stapleton Police Station swearing vengeance amidst her sobs, she soon reneged on her assertion that federal agents were involved. At one point, she claimed it was Eckert's willingness to help everyone that got him into trouble. Mrs. Eckert soon requested federal protection, fearing that her discussion with District Attorney Maloy was misunderstood and that his interpretation of her statements would bring vengeance upon her.

Touring-car owner Charles Kane was soon arrested in connection with the Eckert murder, as was hotel proprietor William Maloney. Both were incarcerated as material witnesses. Maloney's wife, Irene, and bartender Frank Donohue were also brought in, but they were released on $100 bail each. For her part, Mrs. Maloney added a colorful account of Eckert. Two nights before his murder, he was looking for a certain prohibition agent, saying that "if he came across the man, he would 'keep the police busy picking bullets out of his bones.'" By August 25, Max Katz, one of Eckert's stolen liquor drivers, was also in custody. At each arraignment in the old Stapleton Park courthouse, still standing and referred to as the Village Hall in Tappen Park, "witnesses, lawyers and defendants had to fight their way through thousands of Islanders who flocked to the building to listen in. They stood shoulder-to-shoulder on the lawn as the hearings were held."[50]

On a broader level, notice was served on August 27, 1920, that U.S. Attorney Leroy Ross was calling a federal grand jury investigation into wholesale violations of the federal Prohibition laws in Staten Island. On this same day, Richmond County District Attorney William Maloy stated that he was not concerned with violation of Prohibition law, as he would turn over any relative evidence to Ross. He went on to note that he had no reason to look into the conduct of truckman William P. Tiernan, brother of county judge J. Harry Tiernan (who was Maloy's sponsor in political life). Until recently, William had been a licensed vendor of liquors for medicinal purposes on the island. But his alcohol had been found in various Staten Island saloons, including six barrels of whiskey and five cases of gin found at Henry Hugot's roadhouse. Marks and brands on three of the barrels proved they had once been in the possession of William Tiernan. Original ownership of Tiernan's alcohol was often said to be concealed by federal agents who had seized it from illicit locations. As a result, Tiernan's license to distribute medical liquor was revoked. Tiernan's first cousin Howard was also arrested in Brooklyn on July 26 for transporting alcohol without a permit. Judge Tiernan was quick to note his brother's activity as an ensign in the U.S. Naval Reserves during World War I. He steadfastly maintained his brother's innocence. Governor Al Smith soon called for a federal grand jury investigation into Eckert's murder, while New York City mayor John Hylan requested a replacement for Judge Tiernan at Police Court.

What follows is a strange array of statements and actions by Judge J. Harry Tiernan as to why he was sitting on the Police Court the day Maloney and Kane were arraigned for involvement in the murder of Frederick Eckert. It began when District Attorney Maloy went to Tiernan with a request that he cover the Police Court bench on Tuesday, August 24, 1920. Maloy was concerned that Justice Mullen would release the two since Mullen had been "out" the previous night and was unable to perform his court duties. Maloy and Tiernan proceeded to Mullen's home to request that he adjourn the case for five days, as the district attorney believed it would take that much time to prepare a complaint against the two. Supposedly, Mullen agreed as he exited a car driven by Maloy in company with Tiernan as they drove to the courthouse. Mullen, who was on his way to preside at court, asked to stop at Becker's Drug Store in Stapleton for cigars. Maloy and Tiernan continued to the courthouse, where Tiernan was put on the bench. Supposedly, Mullen was nowhere to be found. Tiernan later said he was doing his job by sitting on the bench and that he wanted to see justice done and the case against Kane and Maloney not dismissed.

Judge Mullen was astounded at further statements made by Tiernan and responded, "I have read with amazement [that]...County Judge Tiernan accused me of being too intoxicated on Tuesday last to preside in the Stapleton Magistrate's Court, and am mystified as to his motives for the same, unless he is endeavoring to make me a scapegoat in order to cover up and divert the attention of the public from some personal matter in which he may be interested or involved. His statement that I was drunk the night before, to use a mild term, is without foundation of fact." Mullen noted that Tiernan "seemed overanxious to sit" on the court while Maloney and Kane were arraigned and that the judge offered his services several times. "I had no knowledge at that time that Judge Tiernan's brother, William, was possibly mixed up in the Eckert affair, so I did not suspect any ulterior motive for Judge Tiernan's anxiety to sit."[51]

Tiernan claimed that, owing to political backlashes, harsh feelings existed on Staten Island. From his summer home at Cedar Grove Beach, Tiernan declared, "I have been made the goat long enough, and I am not going to let them make me the goat any longer."[52] He believed it was a grave injustice that his name had been mentioned in connection with the Eckert case.

William P. Tiernan, brother of the judge, was arraigned on August 30, 1920. Pleading not guilty to selling illegal whiskey and falsifying whiskey sales records, even though ample evidence existed to convict both Tiernan and Hugot, the two were released in February 1921. Tiernan's attorney, Alex Drescher, said the indictment was "defective." Held for twenty days, Kane and Maloney were finally freed on September 8, 1920, owing to lack of evidence.

Friction between District Attorney Maloy and U.S. Attorney Leroy Ross resulted when Maloy withheld evidence about the Eckert murder and its bootlegging connections while Ross was investigating Prohibition violations on the island. In response to Maloy's lax attitude, Ross declared, "I am not in the least pleased with Mr. Maloy's conduct in this case."[53]

With very little fanfare, First Assistant District Attorney Alfred Norton announced that a Richmond County grand jury would investigate the Eckert murder. Norton proclaimed that the private grand jury would solve the mystery. Judge J. Harry Tiernan swore in the grand jury on October 4, 1920.

Eckert's murder did lead to an investigation of stolen vehicles moving illegal booze throughout New York and New Jersey. Eckert's right-hand man, Frank Walsh, identified the police officers involved and gave the names of automobile repair shops that harbored stolen cars and illicit whiskey. Other bandits who participated were also tagged. Labeled a "stool pigeon," Walsh was repaid by execution with a bullet through the eye on February 10, 1921.

A new twist in the case came on February 15, 1921, when Russell Brice was indicted in the death of Eckert. Already imprisoned on a conviction of burglary, Brice was not accused of the murder but of being in the car when Eckert was shot. It was believed that Brice was used by the murderer to lure Eckert into the automobile on that fateful night. Known on Staten Island by the alias Jack Whalen, he was associated with Eckert's New Jersey automobile fence operation and was Eckert's accomplice when the two busted through the New Jersey jail wall. Like other hoods, Brice had a number of names on police records, including Jack Dawson, Jack O'Neill and Jack Thompson.

By 1965, the indictment (listed against all of Brice's names, along with two individuals not named to that year) still stood, but the warrant was recalled in 1928 since District Attorney Albert Fach did not have enough evidence to convict Brice. Brice later bragged, "There were only half a dozen of us who made money [during Prohibition]. The rest were boobs. Why, we had so many stolen automobiles we didn't know what to do with them. Many's the night I dropped $500 or $1,000 at a poker game."[54] By 1951, Brice's whereabouts were unknown, as was the killer of Frederick Eckert.

Chapter 8
LIFE FOR THE MURDERER, DEATH FOR COMPLICITY

The four-day period commencing Friday, October 9, 1920, was a particularly crime-ridden time for New York City. Three people died. One was near death. Seven robberies were committed, and thirteen people were under arrest.

The action started early on Staten Island the morning of October 11. Career criminals Frank Eccobacci and Anthony Paoluccio, along with two other men, demanded restaurant receipts from Walter Jaskowski at 2886 Richmond Terrace in Mariner's Harbor. He refused. Instead, Jaskowski lunged across the lunch counter toward the thieves. He was shot in mid-air. The thugs escaped by automobile with all of forty dollars. Meanwhile, Walter Jaskowski was dead.

This was not their first crime of the day. New Brighton resident Andrew Lombardi, a peddler on his way to market by truck, was robbed by the bandits that morning. This effort netted $170. Held at gunpoint by three revolvers, the man who removed the money from Lombardi's pocket threw coins at his feet and told him to go buy breakfast.

Still on the loose, Eccobacci and Paoluccio were plying their trade once again on December 10, 1920. With two other thieves, they were arrested in Stratford, Connecticut. Trucker Luciano Farina was driving along when he came upon four men standing around a disabled car. Farina watched as one of the ruffians drew a gun and demanded he tow their auto. When he refused, the three others produced revolvers, which they promptly pointed at the truck driver. The gunmen were unaware that a nearby farmer had telephoned police with the result that two officers on motorcycles were dispatched. Upon seeing the cops, the thugs ran into the woods. Police followed, firing several shots, which caused the men to surrender. But the illegal activity of the day was not complete. Two of the criminals pulled out stashes of bills and offered the officers bribes for their release. The police refused, and Frank Eccobacci and Anthony Paoluccio were placed under arrest along with Charles Russo and Harry Rega. The latter's pocket held several letters addressed to him at the Blackwell Island prison. He had been released only the day before. Two days later, on December 12, the same four individuals were arraigned in a Bronx court on charges of stealing a car. The theft was witnessed by a policeman.

Authorities eventually traced Frank Eccobacci and Anthony Paoluccio to the murder of Walter Jaskowski in Staten Island. William Connelly and Edward McNally were also arrested for complicity. Initially, Paoluccio admitted he was the killer. When his confession was read at trial, he agreed that he made the confession, but he stated that it was not true—that he had been coerced by threats and beatings at District Attorney Maloy's office. Paoluccio informed the judge that he had the scars to prove it.

Edward McNally's trial began on February 3, 1920, and ended only twenty-four hours later. Found guilty of murder in the first degree, he was sentenced to death by electrocution at Sing Sing Prison the week of March 14 by Justice Callaghan at Saint George Supreme Court. McNally had not even killed Jaskowski; it was Paoluccio who pulled the trigger. He even admitted it again after his initial denial. McNally maintained all along that he knew nothing about the murder of Jaskowski until it occurred. He was to suffer more severely than the actual slayer! William Connelly was given immunity for turning state's evidence against the three, while Paoluccio and Eccobacci were sentenced to serve twenty years to life at Sing Sing. Initially, the two were charged with murder in the first degree, but their jury could not agree, so it was discharged. Immediately thereafter, they pleaded guilty to murder in the second degree and received lighter sentences.

In March 1921, William Connolly went on trial for burglary in Richmond County. One of his cohorts, James Gargone, declared that he, Connolly, Paoluccio, Eccobacci and McNally were part of a group known as the "Crime Association of Staten Island," a band of criminals that robbed and committed offenses relative to Prohibition and bootlegging. Gargone gave clues relevant to the recent murders of Jennie Kussel and Robert Eckert, who were both killed in 1920. The information did nothing to shed light on these still-unsolved cases. Gargone claimed that although Mrs. Kussel had a husband in Jersey City, she often resided at Edward McNally's house and that she and Gargone often visited Staten Island resorts together. For his testimony, Gargone was given immunity on the burglary charge—so anything he said was suspect. When Connelly took the stand, he accused Assistant District Attorney Alfred Norton and Archibald Fulton in the medical examiner's office of bootlegging. He said Norton had hired him to guard whiskey-laden trucks bound for Staten Island saloons, a charge steadfastly denied by Norton.

Judge J. Harry Tiernan slammed Connelly with a fifty-nine-year sentence at Sing Sing for the burglary and stated, "When this fellow gets out, there will be nobody here to receive him who is here today."[55]

McNally's murder conviction was heard by the Court of Appeals on July 15, 1921. The verdict was upheld. As he sat on death row at Sing Sing, McNally did receive some good news. Three of the jurors who convicted him of murder in the first degree had petitioned then-governor Nathaniel Miller to spare his life. Unfortunately, this was countered when word came from McNally's wife that their daughter Meta, who was born during McNally's incarceration, had died.

On August 30, 1921, Governor Miller refused to commute McNally's sentence to life imprisonment. He was to be electrocuted on September 12. Two hours before McNally's scheduled electrocution, dressed in his "death suit" and having had his last meal, word came that he had been given a fifteen-day reprieve by the governor. As the inmates of death row cheered, including two other men scheduled to die that night, McNally sat in disbelief. The two other condemned men were not so fortunate. By midnight, they were dead. The reprieve was granted when Brooklyn judge McCrate issued an order to show cause as to why McNally should not have a new trial. McNally's attorney argued that new evidence regarding the murder had been uncovered. Frank Eccobacci and Anthony Paoluccio both produced affidavits to spare McNally's life. Paoluccio again admitted killing Jaskowski. Thinking he was a man named Lenahan, who had threatened the life of his pal Frank Eccobacci, he had no qualms about killing him. The two flatly stated that McNally knew nothing about the murder. It was not enough. Justice Leander B. Faber of the Brooklyn Supreme Court said the sworn testimony of the two robbers did not warrant a new trial. McNally's wife even went to the Syracuse home of Governor Miller to plead for an execution stay. Miller would not listen, saying that it was "impossible for him to interfere in the carrying out of the law." Mrs. McNally called Miller unjust and said it was all about money, something she and Edward lacked. If she had money for an appeal she believed he would win, "but if you have no money, you lose even though you are innocent."[56] After the refusal, she departed Syracuse for Sing Sing to be with her husband at the end. Warden Lawes informed McNally that he would be put to death that night. McNally was only twenty-two years old.

McNally entered the Sing Sing death chamber at 11:02 p.m. on September 15, 1921. He was pronounced dead by the prison physician at 11:09 p.m. In reality, McNally had died for complicity in the murder of Walter Jaskowski. In a letter to his attorney that was made public on September 16, McNally swore his innocence. Acknowledging that he was guilty of being drunk at the time of the murder, he claimed ignorance about Paoluccio's intent to kill. McNally was appalled that the court would not consider the admissions of Paoluccio and Eccobacci while believing Connelly. But he was taking his fate calmly and making peace with God: "My only regret is the sorrow to the dear one I leave behind, who will have to suffer this disgrace."[57] After a funeral service at the Church of the Assumption in New Brighton, Edward McNally was buried at Silver Mount Cemetery.

Chapter 9

THE BABY FARM MURDER

Dorothy Ennis Johnson was a "baby farmer"—someone who was paid to take and care for another woman's illegitimate child. Usually, these women were unwed mothers, prostitutes or perhaps destitute or deserted wives. It was a lucrative practice. "Farmers" promised mothers that the children would be adopted into loving middle- and upper-middle-class homes. Oftentimes, this did not occur. If it did, the baby farmer made a double profit for taking the infant in and then "farming" it out.

In 1924, a certain Miss Mabel Earle was operating a Staten Island "baby farm," which she did have a license for. Her permit allowed fourteen children on the premises, but the Society for the Prevention of Cruelty to Children reported her to the authorities for having twenty-one youngsters. They ranged in age from fifteen months to fifteen years. At trial, the twenty-six-year-old Earle testified in her defense and admitted threatening the children with a carving knife and telling them that she would cut off their heads and arms if they misbehaved.

Prior to opening a 9 Third Street baby farm in Oakwood, Staten Island, Dorothy Ennis Johnson had operated another farm on Guyon Avenue but was arrested for not possessing a license. Fined fifty dollars, she went on her way and opened another such "business" in the same neighborhood. Licensed or not, Johnson may not have realized at the time that she had a more important issue to deal with. Her real problem was the ending of an illicit relationship with a married man who was a junkie with mental health problems.

It was before noon on June 29, 1927, and Dorothy Ennis Johnson was tending to the children at her unlawful baby farm. There were fourteen children—all between the ages of six months and six years—on the property that day. A friend, Julia Rowley, was visiting. Mrs. Rowley was seated in a chair by a window holding one of the babies when a crazed man burst into the room and fired three shots into Dorothy. She collapsed across a crib, and death soon followed. The shocked Mrs. Rowley clasped the babe to her breast and jumped out the window. Save for a few scratches and bruises, she and the baby were fine. The police arrived so quickly that gun smoke still floated in the nursery while the frightened babies screamed from the chaos. No sooner had Rowley described the killer than officers knew his identity. Well known but not well regarded, Louis P. Heineman was described as dapper yet insignificant, balding and with a sallow complexion. The thirty-two-year-old operated a taxicab stand at Midland Beach. Heineman and Johnson had been having an affair, and after terminating their forbidden relationship, he demanded the return of his clothing. She refused, and a quarrel ensued. Heineman had come to get his clothes—and his revenge—with a loaded .38 caliber pearl-handed revolver. Rusty as it was, it did the job. Ten detectives and twelve uniformed officers fanned out to search for the murderer. Bloodhounds were brought to the scene. They tracked the killer to the Oakwood train station of the Staten Island Rapid Transit line. The trail ended there. Had Louis hopped the train to the Staten Island Ferry and from there gone to parts unknown? Police sent alarms across the country. Photographs and descriptions were distributed. Hundreds of unconfirmed sightings were reported. Imaginative tipsters saw him at local theaters, railroad station platforms and ferry terminals in places as far away as Cuba, California and Tia Juana! There was no trace of Louis P. Heineman. Police believed that since he was a junkie, he would have to surface to find his next fix. They watched his New York City sources and checked addict hangouts. But Louis Heineman never showed himself again.

Police cleaned up the baby farm but were unable to find the waif's mothers. Johnson kept "wonderful" records in not keeping records so that the embarrassed mothers would never be found. The youngsters were sent to Richmond Memorial Hospital and the Society for Prevention of Cruelty to Children in New Brighton.

On October 4, 1927, Louis P. Heineman was indicted for first-degree murder. Heineman's widow believed he was dead. A few days before the shooting, Heineman was so distraught (because of his breakup with Mrs. Johnson) he had attempted suicide by closing himself up in a room with the gas jets on. He was saved when Mrs. Heineman entered the room and closed the jets.

Taxi man Louis Heineman worked out of a stand at popular Midland Beach. Postcard, circa 1910. *Courtesy of Cheryl Criaris-Bontales.*

Louis Heineman was a resident of Stapleton when he killed Dorothy Ennis Johnson at her "baby farm." Postcard, circa 1920s. *Courtesy of Cheryl Criaris-Bontales.*

In 1935, Heineman's widow attempted to get $1,200 of insurance money held in his name. The Surrogate Court refused to acknowledge that he was dead and would allow payment of only $400—the portion of the policy that had been paid up. In order to disburse the remaining $800, she had to prove he was dead, but she could not.

Chapter 10
THE KISS SLAYER

Pretty, intelligent, vibrant and active fifteen-year-old Alice Joost was a popular Port Richmond High School student. Her grades were excellent, as was her reputation, and she was a devout Catholic. One boy who noticed Alice was Vincent Rice, a Curtis High School student who, at that time, was considered to be the all-American boy next door. Tall and handsome with an athletic build, he began seeing Alice on Wednesdays and Sundays with the permission of Mrs. Lucie Joost, Alice's mother. As the deputy street-cleaning inspector, Vincent's father was well known and well regarded on Staten Island. The lives of all concerned would be turned upside down the evening of November 2, 1928.

Lucie Joost and her daughter were expected at the Pelton Avenue home of Mrs. A.W. Brown that Friday night. The previous year, Mrs. Joost's husband passed away. With financial support falling on her shoulders, Lucie took a Manhattan job. On Fridays, Lucie often took dinner with her aunt at the Pelton Avenue address. Alice usually arrived by 8:00 p.m. On this night, Alice did not show up, but Lucie was not too worried. After all, Staten Island was a quiet and safe suburb. When she returned to their Port Richmond home at about 9:30 p.m., Mrs. Joost entered the house without turning on the lights. Entering through a first-floor bedroom, she stumbled across something. Flipping on the lights, Lucie realized she had tripped over Alice's legs. Her daughter was partially on the bed, fully clothed and covered by a pillow and blanket. Hysterically screaming, Lucie Joost ran into the street. When the Richmond County Medical Examiner arrived, Dr. George Mord

Above: "All-American boy" Vincent Rice attended Curtis High School at the time of Alice Joost's murder. *Undated postcard, courtesy of Cheryl Criaris-Bontales.*

Left: The Port Richmond house where Vincent Rice murdered Alice Joost. *Photograph by Patricia M. Salmon, 2013.*

stated that Alice had taken a severe blow to the head but that it hadn't killed her. She had died from strangulation by an electrical cord removed from an iron. The bright red dress Alice wore that day was covered in blood, as were the carpet, stairs and hall. This was a particularly vicious crime.

Even though the Joosts lived in a side-by-side duplex, the immediate neighbors heard only the sound of a piano and singing that day. With few clues to follow, police talked to Alice's friends about the boys she knew. This brought their attention to Vincent Rice, who was questioned the very night of the killing. Rice was released but was brought to the scene of the crime with his father and his brother Orin the following day.

"Standing in front of a crucifix in Alice's room, under which the girl was slain, Mr. Rice urged his son to tell the truth. The boy broke into tears"[58] and fully confessed to killing the young woman. But he had not killed her for just any reason; he killed Alice because she attempted to kiss him! The district attorney contended that Rice had raped her and then murdered her so that the initial crime would not be exposed, but that theory was abandoned when toxicology and other postmortem tests showed that Alice was not raped. A former Staten Island assistant district attorney, Frank Innes represented Vincent Rice. Innes quickly declared Alice's murder the work of a lunatic. Innes, along with the boy's family, thought Vincent was quite mentally unbalanced, so the family retained the best alienist (a psychiatrist with a background in mental health laws). Innes went on to explain that if warranted, a "lunacy commission" would be appointed to determine the teenager's sanity.

Three weeks before he murdered Alice, Rice told authorities they had gone to a party and that she had done something to "displease" him. Friends encouraged him to forget what happened, so he and Alice were to meet in front of the Ritz Theater on Tuesday, October 30. However, she did not appear, and that upset Vincent terribly, so he went to her house on November 2 to meet her before school. They sat and talked, and he spent the next ten hours with her in the house. They discussed All Souls Day Mass, she played the piano and he sang, they had clam chowder for lunch and then they discussed their quarrel. About 5:00 p.m., Alice attempted to put her arms around Vincent and kiss him while saying, "Be a good sport." The endeavor to kiss him and her words "sent him into a rage," so he struck her. Falling, her head caught the pointed edge of a dresser. A horrible scalp wound and unconsciousness followed. He leaned over to pick her up. "Her arms fell limply," and "then he kissed her." At that point, Rice calmly walked through three rooms to the rear of the house, where he located an iron. He ripped the cord from it, "returned to the unconscious girl, wound it about her neck, and tied a loose end to the leg of the chair."[59] Rice wrapped the cord around her neck four times. A number of witnesses saw him calmly departing the house in a brown trench coat. The garment helped the identification process. Police were further assisted when Mrs. Joost informed them that Rice was infatuated with her daughter.

Vincent Rice was indicted for murder in the first degree, but his trial was delayed because District Attorney Albert Fach was preoccupied with trying to put Harry Hoffman behind bars for the murder of Maude Bauer. Hoffman's trial was soon switched to Brooklyn, thus making room for Vincent Rice in the Richmond County Jail.

On November 6, 1928, Alice Joost was buried at Saint Peter's Roman Catholic Cemetery in West New Brighton. Two thousand individuals, including classmates, friends and relatives, were in attendance. One individual missing was the priest who said her requiem funeral Mass at Saint Mary's of the Assumption Roman Catholic Church in Port Richmond, Reverend John B. Snyder. After waiting for the priest, Lucie Joost became hysterical, and with that, woman after woman broke down and wept at the overwhelming sadness of the situation. "Finally the white casket was lowered into the grave. The six pallbearers, schoolmates of Alice, threw their white gloves after it, and the grave diggers began their work."[60]

At the county jail, Rice gained a reputation of being aloof, calm and undisturbed about the murder, Alice's funeral or anything else. His only interaction with guards was to inquire how long he would be incarcerated if found guilty. At the arraignment, he was "nonchalant" and "nattily" dressed in a "snappy overcoat," appearing "more like an interested spectator than one about to be arraigned on a capital charge."[61]

Vincent Rice was examined by two well-known psychiatrists: Dr. George Kirby and Dr. William Pritchard. Both declared Rice was legally sane when he committed the murder, thus Innes's defense was demolished.

Shackled to Richmond County sheriff William S. Hart and Deputy Sheriff Patrick Santry, Rice was brought to Saint George Supreme Court to stand trial on December 17, 1928. Justice Selah B. Strong presided. As Rice waited for the trial to begin, he was cheerful, smiling and laughing. In his dress and manner, he resembled a tall, slim high school football player rather than a murderer fighting for his life. It should be remembered that New York State still had corporal punishment at this time.

The jury box was filled in one hour. Three men were excused because they did not believe in the death penalty. Medical Examiner George Mord

Top: Entrance to Saint Peter's Cemetery, final resting place of Alice Joost. *Photograph by Patricia M. Salmon, 2013.*

Bottom: Alice Joost's funeral Mass at Saint Mary of the Assumption Church was followed by her burial at Saint Peter's Cemetery. *Photograph by Patricia Salmon, 2013.*

was the first to testify. He informed the court that the electrical cord around Alice's neck was so tight that it had broken her skin. After Mrs. Joost took the stand, District Attorney Fach offered the most damaging testimony: Vincent Rice's signed confession to killing his fifteen-year-old sweetheart. No sooner was this read than defense attorney Frank Innes turned to the judge and accepted a previously offered second-degree murder charge. Innes introduced alienist Dr. George Kirby, who "testified that the defendant was retarded in his psychic sexual development and that the boy's act of wrapping the cord around the girl's neck, after he had knocked her down, was unpremeditated."[62] Kirby also stated that "the boy was abnormal and had a constitutional sense of inferiority which had retarded his development." Furthermore, Rice's "emotions were limited," and he was "stubborn, self-willed and lacked deep feeling." In addition, Rice was "subject to depression" but "was abnormally cheerful" when questioned about the murder.[63] Finally, it was noted that he had "a purity complex which rendered him psychopathically abnormal." His response to Alice's kiss attempt had led him to murder. The alienist further believed that Rice had "an impulsive terror of intimacy with girls—probably the effect of a too intensive religious training on a backward mind and an undeveloped sexual instinct." He had "an exaggerated horror to a kiss" and was "repressed sexually, afraid of girls, and afraid that to kiss them might cause him serious physical harm." Rice went so far as to tell Dr. Kirby that he "struck the deceased in order to protect his honor and preserve his health." According to Dr. Kirby, "Somewhere…the boy had acquired a real fear of intimacy with girls, which would explain his abhorrence when…the girl attempted to kiss him."[64]

Rice pleaded guilty to second-degree murder and was sentenced to twenty years to life at Sing Sing. Eligibility for parole would not occur until twenty years had been served. Vincent Rice showed no emotion when Judge Strong read the verdict. When asked if he had anything to say, his lips formed a soundless no. On December 27, 1928, Vincent Rice was driven to Sing Sing Prison to begin his sentence for murdering Alice Joost.

Chapter 11

THE MOVIE PROJECTIONIST MURDERER?

On March 25, 1924, Maude Bauer, along with her mother, Catherine Pero, and her three-year old daughter attempted to visit a relative in Bloomfield. As they traveled along Merrill Avenue (a road historically and ironically known as the "Long, Long Road That Has No End"), Maude's car was propelled off the road by an oncoming truck. Stuck in a ditch, she was unable to budge the car. Before Mrs. Pero could stop her, Maude took off on foot down the road to find a good Samaritan with a rope who would pull the car free. She hadn't gone far along South Avenue when a dark car with a swarthy, robust man pulled over. Innocently, she got in the car with the stranger. That was the last time anyone saw Maude Bauer alive. Within ten minutes, four boys came upon her lifeless body. She had been shot once in the neck and once in the abdomen. With two bullet holes, Maude and her pocketbook had been hastily tossed to the side of the road.

An attractive thirty-one-year-old woman, Mrs. Bauer had no enemies. She had been misled by a depraved individual who promised assistance but gave grave harm. No doubt she struggled greatly, owing to the disarray of her clothing. Her brother, the Reverend Addison Pero, stated in the *New York Times* of April 20, 1924, "I believe the man made an insulting remark. Hardly had the words left his lips than he began to receive his punishment at the hands of my sister." Assuming the posture of the boxer, Reverend Pero demonstrated for reporters how his sister must have reacted. "Maude struck him in the face. It wasn't a slap or a scratch, but one of the real blows she knew how to deliver." According to Pero, "she had learned how to box and

Far left: Murder victim Maude L. Bauer, circa 1923. *Courtesy of* The Saratogian, *March 29, 1924.*

Left: Harry L. Hoffman before imprisonment. *Courtesy of* The Saratogian, *April 23, 1924.*

had developed a formidable punch." Two neighborhood lads, sixteen-year-old Ernest Van Clief and seventeen-year-old George Carlson, reported seeing Mrs. Bauer step into a Ford sedan driven by a man in a brown coat and brown hat. Five other children corroborated this recollection, but it was thirteen-year-old Barbara Fahs of Merrill Avenue who heard the driver say to Mrs. Bauer, "Come on. Jump in. I'll drive you to the nearest garage, and we can get a rope."[65] Brought in for questioning was Harry L. Hoffman, but Barbara Fahs was unable to identify Hoffman in person (it was later discovered that he had altered his appearance). However, she did identify him through a photograph. Hoffman's Ford sedan was identified by a group of workmen cutting trees near the murder site. They had been hired by Horatio J. Sharrett, a well-known realtor and insurance man who owned property in the area. Sergeant Matthew McCormick also witnessed Hoffman driving from the direction of South Avenue in a Ford sedan shortly after Mrs. Bauer was killed.

Authorities received a number of letters regarding the murder. Some came from as far away as Texas. One came from a spiritualist who believed she knew the identity of the murderer. But the investigation soon focused on film projectionist Harry L. Hoffman, who worked at the Palace Theatre in Port Richmond. Initially, Hoffman stated that he was with fellow movie projectionist Racey Parker at the time of the murder. With support from Parker, Hoffman said he was checking on a new style of movie projector used at the Liberty Theatre in Stapleton. Unfortunately for Hoffman, neither the theater ticket taker nor theater manager William Taylor could corroborate his presence. Eventually, Hoffman's alibi fell completely apart, especially after Parker denied Hoffman's presence in the projection room on March 25, which incidentally was a Tuesday, Hoffman's usual day off. Parker admitted to police that Hoffman had pleaded with him to verify his visit to the Liberty Theatre on that date. When Detective Timothy Cotter went to the Liberty Theatre to escort Parker back to the office of District Attorney Fach (who ironically owned a share of the theater), Cotter encountered Harry Hoffman's younger sibling David. When questioned about his presence at the Liberty Theatre, David replied that he was there at the behest of Hoffman's wife, who wanted Parker "not to take the District Attorney's 'guff' and to keep his mouth shut."[66]

Hoffman's next alibi put him on the Saint George-to-Manhattan ferry at the time of Maude's murder. After a stop at his broker's office, an aborted trip to the oriental restaurant on Pell Street in Chinatown for chop suey and a stop at another Chinese restaurant on Sixth Avenue, Hoffman claimed he returned to Staten Island via the 4:00 p.m. Staten Island ferry. There were no witnesses to Hoffman's activities, so he lied and pleaded with Parker to back him up with the fictitious theater visit.

On April 18, 1924, Harry Hoffman was charged with the vicious murder of Maude Bauer. Circumstantial evidence was piling up against Hoffman. He had purchased a .25 caliber Colt pistol from Abercrombie and Fitch under an assumed name prior to the murder. (Because he was a deputy sheriff in his spare time, Hoffman was able to pick up the gun from the Port Richmond Post Office even though it was addressed to an L. Rothman.) Then, four days after the murder, Hoffman inexplicably mailed the weapon to his brother Albert in Manhattan. Hoffman claimed to have burned the gun's holster, stating that he simply did not want it around the house, but police theorized he destroyed it because it held the stains of Maude Bauer's blood. After the killing, Hoffman cut his hair noticeably shorter and began wearing "nose glasses" (pince-nez glasses) instead of his usual tortoise-shell pair. Suspicion of Hoffman was further aroused when he announced to Harry Edkins, assistant projectionist at the Palace Theatre, that he was being investigated for the murder of Maude Bauer. This announcement occurred on March 26, long before the police had any suspect. It was after mentioning this to Edkins that Hoffman declared the need for a haircut. As he left for the barber, he told Edkins to find someone to paint his Ford sedan.

In their investigation, police located two women who declared they had been attacked by Harry Hoffman. Both were offered rides in his Ford sedan and then driven to a lonely destination, where he threatened them with a pistol. Hoffman was indicted on attempted felonious assault for the attack of Mrs. Catherine Campbell during October 1923. On leaving the Staten Island Ferry terminal at Saint George during a driving rainstorm, Mrs. Campbell, without raincoat or umbrella, was waiting for a trolley to take her home when a man fitting Hoffman's description drove up in his Ford sedan and offered her a ride. She declined, but after additional discussion, she accepted his offer and climbed into the back seat. According to Campbell, the man drove to a desolate area and menaced her with a gun but then switched to small talk, telling her he worked at the Palace Theatre and that perhaps they knew mutual people.

Held at the Richmond jail during the investigation and indictment, after two weeks, Hoffman was growing impatient. In late April, he requested a speedy trial, later saying, "Jail was no place for an innocent man."[67]

The trial was held before Judge J. Harry Tiernan at the Saint George Supreme Court. The jury received the case at 6:30 p.m. on May 28, 1924. Represented by attorney Alfred V. Norton, Hoffman was brought to the stand, and under cross-examination, the usually stoic Hoffman became emotional and accused District Attorney Albert Fach of lying when he intimated that the pistol holster was destroyed because it was spattered with the blood of Maude Bauer's battered head.

Some 2,500 men, women and children awaited the verdict outside the Saint George courtroom. It arrived at 7:05 a.m.—twelve and a half hours after it was received by the jury. Harry L. Hoffman was found guilty of murdering Maude Bauer. Hoffman collapsed as the foreman announced the verdict. Judge Tiernan sentenced Hoffman to twenty years to life and ordered him to Sing Sing Prison. As Undersheriff Peter Finn led him out of the courtroom, Hoffman flew into a rage, and turning to Fach, he screamed, "Go out and split up the huge reward with your bunch of lying witnesses. You know Fach, I am as innocent as you are." With that, the district attorney replied, "Hoffman, it would be unbecoming of me to enter into a discussion with you at this time."[68] While Hoffman was shipped off to "Murderer's Row" at the jail in Richmond, his mother was brought in the following morning. She had not been told of her son's plight until a few minutes before arriving. Hoffman swore he was innocent, and his mother responded, "I believe you, my boy."[69]

Not much was going right for Harry L. Hoffman, but in February 1927, his situation changed. The Appellate Division found Hoffman's conviction on murder in the second degree faulty, so it was overturned and he was re-indicted for murder in the first degree.

On March 5, 1928, Harry L. Hoffman once again stood before Judge Tiernan on the charge of murdering Maude Bauer. This time, he was defended by Leonard A. Snitkin, who had had a number of spirited clashes with both the judge and district attorney. The trial came to a surprising halt on March 19 when Snitkin collapsed from a heart attack. Convalescing at Lakewood, New Jersey, for a week, Snitkin returned to the courtroom on March 26. After a heated argument with Fach, Snitkin headed for Tiernan's bench, but he didn't make it. Instead, the lawyer collapsed on the prosecutor's table. Tiernan declared a mistrial. After a three-week rest in South Carolina, Snitkin returned to New York City on April 15, 1928, and quickly called for a third trial. On May 1, Snitkin appeared before Justice Dunne in Kings County Supreme Court to request a Brooklyn venue for the next Hoffman trial. Declaring that "a thumbs-down sentiment exists on Staten Island towards Harry Hoffman," Snitkin told Dunne, "If your Honor sends this man to a trial in Richmond County, you are signing his death warrant. They hate him there. He has no more chance of a fair trial there than I would have if I were to be tried in a southern Ku Klux Klan territory"[70] (Leonard Snitkin was Jewish). The request was granted, and Harry Hoffman's third trial opened in Kings County Supreme Court on November 7, 1928. Justice Stephen Callaghan presided over a "blue-ribbon" panel of jurors selected from 150 individuals. Since the first trial, Hoffman had wasted away from a healthy 190 pounds to a scant 114 pounds, and his wife had remarried. At this trial, the prosecution produced ex-wife Agnes Rankin. At the close of a severe cross-examination by Snitkin, she fell to the floor screaming. Removed from the court, she was calmed in an adjacent chamber.

On November 23, 1928, Harry Hoffman took the stand in his own defense. Calm, quiet and patient throughout his six-hour examination, he remained so even when District Attorney Fach brought in his ex-wife. According to a newspaper account, "Mr. Fach suddenly shouted at him, 'Did you ever horse whip your wife at Lover's Lane because of a quarrel over a tenant?'" Hoffman denied it. Fach then asked, "Did you ever, on any occasion, tie her to a tree and beat her?" Again, Hoffman denied the allegation. Mrs. Catherine Campbell was then brought forth, and Hoffman was asked if he had ever threatened her with a gun after offering her a ride home on a rainy night in October 1923. He denied it. Fach then brought a Mrs. Simon into the courtroom and emphatically asked Hoffman if he had taken her into his Ford sedan against her wishes during late 1923.[71] The question was never answered, as counselor Snitkin voiced an objection, which was sustained. In closing, Snitkin proclaimed Hoffman to be the victim of a "police frame-up," while Fach contended that the defendant had "shown himself to be an unmitigated liar" and that the "whole case offered by the defense is saturated with perjury."[72]

The public was astonished when the jury returned to the courtroom on November 27, 1928—they could not agree on a verdict. Justice Callaghan declared a mistrial, and the jurors were released. Hoffman returned to the Raymond Street jail in Brooklyn, and Snitkin called for his discharge on bail. Prosecutor Fach would have none of it and instead called for a new trial in the ruthless murder of Maude Bauer.

By January 19, 1929, the ailing Leonard Snitkin was dead from heart disease, and even though Harry L. Hoffman was penniless, he wrote attorney Samuel Leibowitz requesting his representation. Leibowitz agreed.

Promising the speediest trial for Hoffman yet, Brooklyn Supreme Court Justice Humphrey presided. From the beginning, Leibowitz argued that someone else had committed the crime and that Hoffman had been framed. On May 7, 1929, Leibowitz boldly announced that Horatio J. Sharrett was the real murderer. Realtor Sharrett was the property owner whose woodchoppers were cutting trees in Bloomfield the day Maude Bauer was murdered. Well respected on the island, Sharrett had previously stated he was in the area checking on the workers' progress. From an old Staten Island family, Sharrett was the brother of Republican leader Clinton J. Sharrett. It was hinted that Sharrett's political connections shielded his guilt. Leibowitz stressed that Sharrett was heavyset, wore horn-rimmed glasses and drove a Ford sedan. Leibowitz also went to great lengths to stress that Hoffman was left-handed and that the Colt's safety device would have made it difficult for him to fire the weapon.

Fifty-nine-year-old Horatio Sharrett went before the court on May 13, 1929, and thoroughly described his actions and whereabouts the day of the murder. Nothing startling was reported or alluded to. Once again, Barbara Fahs, now eighteen years old, took the stand. After stating that it was Hoffman and his Ford that she saw, Leibowitz cast doubt on her memory by asking for previously attended school numbers, prior house addresses and the exact date of the first trial. None of these questions was assuredly answered.

The defense began its case with a report from Albert Foster of the Colt Patents Firearms Company, who stated that the bullets found in Maude Bauer's body did not correspond with the rifling of Hoffman's Colt .25. Former New York City police captain William Jones verified his findings. Fach had previously brought in ballistic experts to confirm that Hoffman's gun fired the fatal bullets. In a final dramatic move, Hoffman took the stand

Far left: The defense attempted to blame realtor Horatio J. Sharrett for the murder of Maude Bauer. *From* Prominent Men of Staten Island, *1893.*

Left: Movie projectionist Harry L. Hoffman was tried four times for the murder of Maude Bauer. *Courtesy of* The Saratogian, *March 29, 1924.*

and pleaded for death or freedom. In addition to his wife's divorce and losing his children, Hoffman stated that five years in prison was enough, especially for a crime he did not commit. The trial closed with Harry Hoffman stating emphatically that he had never fired the .25-calibre Colt pistol and that he was entitled to own a weapon since he was a deputy sheriff. He implored the judge and the jury to believe that his left-handedness made it impossible for him to successfully shoot the gun.

A pallid, trembling Harry Hoffman walked into Justice Humphrey's courtroom on the arm of his attorney just before 9:00 p.m. on May 22, 1929. The jury had reached a verdict. Appearing in danger of collapse, Hoffman waited as jury foreman Reginald C. Thomas announced, "We find the defendant not guilty." The stunned courtroom was in silence as Hoffman, with tears in his eyes, embraced Leibowitz.

In the reporter's room afterward, Agnes Rankin, Hoffman's common-law wife, announced she would divorce her current husband to be with Harry again. "I haven't an idea what Harry will do, but I guess he can get a job somehow." Owing to her desertion and the neglect of their children while he was jailed, Hoffman declined her offer. Hoffman's luck was changing. The Motion Pictures Operator's Union, of which he was a member, found him a new job at a Times Square theater. He could begin a few weeks after recuperation in the Adirondacks courtesy of the same organization. Leibowitz, too, revealed that he had donated his services free of charge because he believed Harry was getting a rough deal. Of Harry's odd behavior after the murder of Maude Bauer, Leibowitz said, "It was compromising... due to the influence of motion pictures on his client."[73] District Attorney Fach disgustedly stated that further charges against Harry Hoffman would not be pressed.

Sad to say that the month before her murder, Maude and her husband, Walter, closed a lease on a Rutherford, New Jersey home. They were planning to move to their new residence in April, the month after Maude's cruel murder. No one was ever punished for the murder of Maude Bauer.

Chapter 12
THAT MOST WICKED AND WRETCHED WOMAN

Perhaps the most consuming unsolved Staten Island mystery is the oft-discussed and much-analyzed murder of Emeline and Ann Eliza Housman. The accused killer lays in a grave at Fairview Cemetery at Four Corners, unmarked for over one hundred years. Mary "Polly" Bodine was vilified by the Staten Island community—then and even to this day. This is the story of the arson, murder and the accused murderer.

The Housman residence was a snug two-story shuttered cottage built by George Housman around 1841 in Graniteville. It still stands today on a seldom-used section of Richmond Avenue that is set apart from the main thoroughfare. Surrounded by a traditional white wooden railing, the house sat on property owned by George's father, Abraham, who made a comfortable living and later realized a real estate windfall when he sold his farm to the Staten Island Granite Company. In fact, his house was separated from George's by only a fence and a small garden. There were two rooms on the first floor of the George Housman house. One was a parlor and the other a kitchen. This is where the notorious slaughter took place.

Christmas Eve 1843 was a violently stormy evening, with the wind twisting and roiling the trees that surrounded the Housman property. The following evening, Christmas night, at about 9:30 p.m., Jesse Clark's landlady ordered him to run and hallo fire, as the Housman house was burning. When the fire was finally extinguished, Isaac Cruzer raked the embers and was horrified to find the body of twenty-four-year-old Emeline Housman, wife of George Housman and mother of his child. Cruzer then screamed, "Here is the corpse!"

fled the building and refused to enter again until the deceased was removed. It did strike Cruzer that the woman had purposely been placed under the bed. It was strange, too, that the floor around her body was not burned. It was Daniel Crocheron who uncovered the remains of George and Emeline's daughter, Ann Eliza, who was only one year and eight months old. Not far from her mother, the floor around the child was also unburned. This indicated that both were dead before the fire had been started. While examining the burned debris shoveled into the basement, a piece of the child's skull was found. Part of the scalp was bloody and reddish, but the attached hair was not singed—another indication that the child was dead before the blaze occurred. In fact, this fire burned so hot that it left the kitchen blackened with raised heat blisters on all surfaces. It was further found that all the doors (except the front door) of the Housman cottage were locked and bolted.

As the day progressed, the house turned into a sideshow, with carriage loads of gawkers coming to see the site where Emeline and her daughter were murdered and burned. Memorabilia of the horror was carted off, with pieces of a handkerchief, a baby shoe, the Housman Bible and even a bedpost seized as macabre reminders of the horror. Much of the material was blackened, thus enhancing the value of each artifact.

The day after the fire, Dr. William G. Eadie examined the deceased and discovered that Mrs. Housman had a forearm wound. Positive that it had been inflicted before the fire, the injury was jagged and had been caused by an obtuse instrument. Eadie also found fractured bones on the left forearm, but he could not verify that the fractures had been made prior to the fire. The back part of Mrs. Housman's skull was also severed. According to Dr. Eadie, this, too, had occurred before the fire. The doctor also found the child's skull filled will blood, thus indicating a terrible violence. Eadie believed that the fire was started two days after Emeline and Ann Eliza were slain.

Emeline's sister-in-law Mary "Polly" Bodine quickly became the prime suspect in the murder and arson. In her youth, Polly was said to be a strong girl with little fear. "She could pull an oar in an oyster boat with any man in the crew. She was quiet, reticent, and never made many friends."[74] It was also said that Polly shunned society. The newspapers of the day painted her as the evil murderess. As such, the community quickly turned against her, with one neighbor stating, "If the law would give her up to the women of the Island, they would hang her without judge or jury." One reporter claimed the citizens were so vehemently opposed to Polly that she could never receive a fair trial on the island. According to the newsman, "Not the angel Gabriel himself could now persuade them to the contrary."[75]

Mary "Polly" Bodine lived an unconventional life for a woman of her time. It did not help that her husband, Andrew Bodine, was a bigamist incarcerated at Sing Sing Prison. First brought to the attention of authorities when his second wife mysteriously died after two hours of marriage, he was charged but not convicted, owing to insufficient testimony. Unbelievably, Andrew Bodine's actions and unlawful behavior were blamed on Polly! It was said that he had been a man of character before he married her and that only thereafter did he become intemperate and worthless. Before they separated, Polly bore two children. In 1844, Albert was sixteen years old, while his sister, Eliza, was one year younger.

Said to be approximately thirty-three years old at the time of the murder, Polly was described as pretty with dark curly hair. Her eyes were attractive and noticeable. More pertinent to the case was that Polly was said to possess a bad character because she lived separately from her husband in a disgraceful manner. At times, when not on Staten Island, Polly lived with pharmacist George Waite at his apothecary shop at 232 Canal Street in Manhattan. Albert Bodine also lived at the location, as he worked in the pharmacy. Polly was further denigrated at the time of the murder because she was pregnant with Waite's child. It was also rumored that she had multiple abortions terminated by drugs provided by George Waite.

Emeline Housman was a timid woman. With a husband who was an oyster-boat captain, she was often alone. As such, she often spent the night with family members or had them stay with her. It soon became the responsibility of Eliza Bodine, Polly's daughter, to spend nights with her aunt to calm her fears. On the Wednesday before the murders, Eliza was sent by Polly to visit the Freemans, who lived some distance from Graniteville. On Thursday, Polly sent a message to her daughter telling her not to return on Friday, as there was considerable mud and she deemed it unsafe for her daughter to travel. This left Polly with the responsibility of staying with Emeline.

Polly swore under oath that she spent the night of Saturday, December 23, with Emeline and that she departed at 6:30 a.m. the following morning for her father's adjacent house. Returning to Emeline's at about 4:00 p.m. on Sunday, December 24, she found the house locked with no one at home, so she went back to her father's home and spent the night with her parents. When she left her father's on Christmas morning, she saw George's house closed and shuttered, so she headed for the 8:00 a.m. ferry to Manhattan. Polly stated that she did not hear of Emeline and Ann Eliza's death until Tuesday, December 26, when Freeman Smith came to Waite's apothecary shop and told her of the horrendous murders. Bursting into tears, Polly

POLLY BODINE.

Above, left: *From* The Era Magazine, *1904.*

Above, right: *From the* New York Herald, *January 8, 1844.*

Right: *From the* National Police Gazette, *May 2, 1848.*

headed for the ferry terminal to get to Staten Island. Ironically, her brother George was on the same boat, so it fell to Polly to tell him about Emeline and Ann Eliza. George had been away for several months and had just docked his schooner on the Hudson River. It was said that Emeline and Ann Eliza were murdered because George had $1,000 in his house from the sale of an oyster schooner. But in reality, the money had been placed in his parent's home, as it made Emeline nervous to keep cash in their residence. It later came to light that Polly was well aware of the money's true location. Early in the investigation, it was stated that the murderer had tortured Mrs. Housman and her babe for the whereabouts of the money. The rumor further turned the public against Polly Bodine.

Suspicion increased after Richmond County District Attorney Lot C. Clarke called on George Housman to discuss the arson and murder. Polly was present but disappeared soon thereafter. At first, her mother and son believed she had committed suicide. Others said she had gone missing and killed herself, owing to guilt. It soon became apparent that Polly had simply returned to Manhattan.

When he commenced the investigation, Clarke had little suspicion that Polly or any other member of the family committed the crimes. But at the conclusion of the Housman family interview, he felt the existence of guilt.

As can be imagined, a massive state of fear over the murders existed on Staten Island. Residents stocked up on bullets and placed loaded shotguns by every door in the event that the killer appeared on their doorstep. Windows were locked, doors were bolted and every visitor, especially strangers, was examined carefully from behind glass. One reporter said that Staten Island was in a state of siege.

One of the last people to see Emeline Housman alive was Polly's sister, Caroline Van Name, who had seen Emeline sweeping out the back of her house at about 10:00 a.m. on the morning of Sunday, December 24. Emeline's niece Matilda Rourke also saw her aunt going from the Housman abode to the woodhouse at about 9:00 a.m. on that Sunday. The woman had her aunt's dress on and had the same stature. Some suggested it was Polly masquerading as Emeline so that witnesses would think the woman was alive, but the niece said she knew the difference between the two. Matilda also stated that when Captain Housman had brought the proceeds from the sale of the boat to her grandmother's house, Polly was there, so Polly knew the money was safeguarded elsewhere.

Suspicion of Polly increased when her male companion, George Waite, was placed on the island on December 23. People believed Waite was an accessory to the crimes because he was in debt. He was further incriminated when Albert Bodine reported a conversation he had with the pharmacist. Albert was told that if anyone questioned Polly's whereabouts on Christmas Day, the boy should answer that she slept with Waite at the shop, even though Waite and Albert slept in the same bed. In addition, he was ordered to say that she had not left the store for more than ten or fifteen minutes on Christmas Day.

On Saturday, December 30, Polly let a room near Waite's shop from Lena Parsells on Washington Street in Manhattan. At about 9:00 p.m., word came from Mrs. Parsells that constables were searching Waite's pharmacy. Visibly upset, Polly requested that the landlady not tell the officers she was in Parsells's house. Jumping out of bed, she quickly dressed, paid Mrs. Parsells and said she was headed to Waite's to see what all the fuss was about. Parsells later heard that Polly was seen crying as she walked in the *opposite* direction of Waite's establishment.

Polly Bodine was arrested in Manhattan on December 31 for the murders of Emeline and Ann Eliza Housman. Brought before the magistrate at the police office on Centre Street, she was very distraught and proclaimed her innocence. A pawnbroker swore she was the woman who pawned a watch at his shop. The watch belonged to George Housman. A basket maker named Charles Arcombe also identified Polly as the woman who brought a basket into his Spring Street, Manhattan shop for repair on Christmas Day. The basket belonged to Emeline Housman. Mrs. Bodine picked up the repaired basket the following day. Other missing items owned by the Housmans included a gold chain, which was found at Levi's pawnshop on East Broadway in Manhattan; six table spoons later located at Hart's pawnshop on Chatham Street; and two dessert spoons and a sugar tong that were pawned at Davis's shop on the same avenue. When the articles were shown to Polly, she identified them as belonging in her brother's home. Worse yet for her, the clerks from each pawnshop identified her as the bearer of the stolen goods. Matilda Rourke would later say that the pawned sugar tongs and spoons were in the Housman house on the afternoon of Saturday, December 23. Several pieces of silverware were engraved "E.H." for Emeline Housman, but the woman who sold them stated that "E. H." stood for Ellen Henderson. Beads seen by Matilda at the Housman house on Saturday were later discovered at Waite's apothecary shop.

Owing to the evidence found at his shop and his December 23 presence on Staten Island, George Waite was charged as an accessory to the Housman house arson. He was arrested on January 3 when he returned to Staten Island with Albert. On January 8, the *New York Herald* wrote that Polly Bodine had seduced a respectable citizen—George Waite—"from the strict path of duty."

Albert informed authorities that when he and Waite passed the Housman house after the murder and fire, Waite was unable to look directly at the abode. A letter found on Waite's person at the time of his arrest was said to be from Polly requesting a particular drug. It was immediately believed that this drug was administered to murder Emeline. Polly's own daughter certified that the note was written in her mother's hand.

Albert also stated that he had met his mother on the first boat from Staten Island to Manhattan on Christmas morning. Arriving at Waite's shop, Albert was immediately sent out to pick up mutton even though there was ample food in the house for the Christmas repast. Misinformation was rampant. On Christmas night, Polly left Waite's saying she was going to visit a woman by the name of Mrs. Strang. When a Staten Island neighbor arrived the following morning to tell Albert of the Housman murders and arson, he sought his mother at Mrs. Strang's. Not only was she not there, but she had not been there the previous night either.

The situation was further heightened and the public's interest piqued on January 6. At 8:00 a.m. that morning, the imprisoned Polly Bodine gave birth to George Waite's child. Two to three weeks premature, he was stillborn. Polly was said to be physically well after the birth.

Polly Bodine was to appear at the Court of Inquiry on January 15, 1844, but owing to what was described as a "fit," the appearance was postponed. "She raved incessantly, calling at various times upon Waite to come and untie her; that she did not know what she was confined for, [while she made] other incoherent expressions."[76] The newspapers insinuated that this was a preliminary performance to a plea of insanity.

On January 20, Polly finally appeared before the Court of Inquiry. Described as pale and feeble, she kept her eyes focused on the ground. Through her attorney, she pleaded not guilty to the crimes of murder, arson and felony.

The trial of Mary "Polly" Bodine and George Waite began on Monday, June 24, 1844. With Judge Parker and four associate judges on the bench, the trial was held at the Richmond County Courthouse. From the start, one of the jurors, James Decker, posed problems. First, he refused to take an oath of affirmation. The judge offered him time to reflect on his actions but warned that if he continued to refuse, he would be confined for contempt. Decker obstinately responded that he did not care and that since his money had helped build the jail, he would be only too willing to stay in it. As such, a recess was taken. When the court reassembled, Decker announced a change of heart and took his oath of affirmation. Along with Decker, the men of the jury were from some of Staten Island's oldest families. They included Henry DeHart, Henry S. Seguine, James Totten, Daniel Simonson, John LaForge and John Lake.

Richmond County Courthouse, the site of the John Bell and Edward Reinhardt trials, as well as the first Polly Bodine court case. *Photograph by Patricia M. Salmon, 2013.*

Polly Bodine was then brought in to the courtroom. She looked no worse for the incarceration, and some even remarked that she looked much better. She pleaded not guilty. At trial, Abram Whitelay reported seeing a red mark around the neck of Emeline Housman, and Daniel Crocheron corroborated his early testimony of finding the dead child. Dr. William G. Eadie reported that the brain of Emeline Housman was exposed and scorched by the fire and that both forearm bones were broken and a flesh wound was present. He reported that some of the child's head bones were gone and that some of the remaining brain was unburned. Eadie reiterated that Emeline's body had been burned after death and that the child's injuries were inflicted prior to the fire. Neighbor Ann Shotwell was then called to the stand. Her testimony supported the theory that mother and daughter were killed before the fire, as she had seen bloodied muslin, flannel and a section of carpet at the scene of the crime. Shotwell had not previously told anyone about the blood-covered materials, owing to modesty. It was her first belief that it was "relative to the female sex."

The letter that Polly wrote to George Waite contained some of the most damning testimony. In part, it read, "You will be examined concerning my coming to New York on Monday. You and Albert must say that Albert came to the Jersey ferry for me, and I remained with you all day, with the exception of fifteen minutes, when I went to Spring Street to get a basket mended. Come to the island—you will be treated well. The store and all is going to be searched. Hide the things where they cannot be found."[77]

George Housman took the stand and, under oath, stated that the sale of the schooner had netted $1,000. He verified that when he gave it to his mother for safekeeping, Polly was present. George's mother then took the stand and swore that Polly and Emeline were on the most affectionate terms.

On July 5, 1844, the twelve men of the jury came in with a verdict of eleven guilty and one not guilty. At the beginning of deliberation, eight called Polly guilty and four not guilty, so Judge Parker sent them back to reach a unanimous decision, but they could not concur. Without a verdict, a second trial was necessary. The dissenting juror was James Decker, who had originally troubled the court by refusing the oath of affirmation. Decker had actually been brought up on charges after the trial's first day. Instructing the jury to stay together for the entire night, the sheriff locked the men up in a room. Decker would have none of it, so he jumped out a window and went home. Regarding the verdict, it was Decker's opinion that the evidence presented did not warrant a guilty verdict. As such, Decker invented the "doctrine of circumstantial evidence in the fourth degree," as he was not for any verdict based on circumstantial evidence unless it was circumstantial evidence that had four eyewitnesses "who would swear that they saw the act committed."[78]

Polly Bodine could not receive a fair trial in Staten Island, so the second took place in Manhattan. At court, she was attended by her counsel, parents, children and other relatives when the ordeal began on March 20, 1845. Subsequently, her brother George, Emeline's husband and father of Ann Eliza, sat with the family in support of Polly. The courtroom was filled to the maximum with spectators. This included crowds of females. More people were interested in this trial than had been in any other for years. The proceedings were said to resemble a theater debut as opposed to a court case with a woman fighting for her life. Indeed, the trial was discussed everywhere, both in and out of New York City.

After an arduous deliberation, the men of the jury reached their verdict on April 12, 1845—it was guilty but with a recommendation of mercy. Polly sat stoically as the decision was read, but nothing could equal the excitement that spread far and wide.

On May 28, 1845, Clinton DeWitt, counsel for Polly Bodine, submitted a motion for a new trial. Numerous arguments were given for the retrial, including removal of the trial from Richmond County and juror incompetence. On July 10, the courts agreed to a new trial.

With announcement of a third trial, the *New York Daily Tribune* wrote on November 10, 1845, "The fate of this woman has been much more horrible than mere death. To be dragged joint by joint through the sack of the law, her heart all the while bursting with suspense, fear, and hope, and her eye dry with agony—and this month after month, year after year—is infinitely worse than hanging." The saga was referred to by some as a torture worse than punishment received for conviction of a crime. That same month, the *New York Herald* rendered another opinion: "The trial of criminals have become a farce—a solemn mockery and by-word. It is almost impossible to obtain a conviction, be the evidence never so clear. There is no doubt existing of her guilt."

It was impossible to find jurors for the third trial. As such, the venue was switched to Newburgh, New York. It would be heard at the next circuit court, scheduled to commence the first Monday of April 1846. The citizens of Orange County were extremely displeased, owing to the expenses realized at the Manhattan trial. For this reason, they petitioned the legislature for financial relief.

Interestingly, by this third trial, the New York press had grown tired of the case. Supposedly, not one reporter was sent to Newburgh from a New York City newspaper for the third trial.

The trial opened on April 8 to an overflowing Orange County, New York audience. Hundreds were unable to gain admittance. Much emaciated and careworn, Polly was attended by family. The defense team consisted of Messrs. Graham and Jordan. They wisely enlisted the service of Newburgh attorney John W. Brown with the hope that he would have influence over the jury. This was a successful logistical move, as it swung many local residents to Polly's side. District Attorney Lot. C. Clark led the prosecution.

An interesting schism developed amongst the population of Newburgh. With the judge, jury and defense counsel staying in the United States Hotel and the prosecutors lodged in the Orange County House, each hotel took up the cause of its paying guest and became a leader for locals favoring their resident's side.

With great surprise, Polly Bodine was acquitted of murdering Emeline and Ann Eliza Housman on the evening of Saturday, April 18, 1846. Some believe that Polly Bodine was not convicted because the death penalty was considered too harsh for a woman. The following month, Polly Bodine was released from jail.

After the trial, Polly went into semi-seclusion with her son and daughter at 28 Lafayette Avenue in Port Richmond. It was said she practiced medicine

Mary "Polly" Bodine's final residence. *Photograph by Patricia M. Salmon, 2013.*

and that her clients had considerable confidence in her skills. Polly claimed to be afraid of only four things: thunder, lightning, snakes and the Devil.

Many bizarre stories about Polly Bodine and the trials circulated over the years. Some have surfaced recently. A clairvoyant stated that Polly and her mother hired a man to kill Emeline and the baby. It was also claimed that Emeline was pregnant with her second child when she was murdered.

Owing to an increase in unsolved crimes and murders in the New York area, the *New York Herald* of May 15, 1857, proffered various sums of money leading to the conviction of responsible criminals. $5,000 was offered for the person or persons who killed Emeline and Ann Eliza Housman.

In March 1844, promoter P.T. Barnum jumped into the circus surrounding the Housman murders with newspaper announcements inviting the public to view "faithfully represented" wax figures of the infamous Polly Bodine. Inquirers could see the representations for twenty-five cents, while children under ten were admitted for half price. The show was called the American Museum and Perpetual Fair, and it was located at Broadway and Ann Street in Manhattan. As part of the presentation, visitors could see a family of six

"Gipsys" and have their fortune told by the "Gipsy Queen" for an extra twenty-five cents. Signor Francisco, the magician and equilibrist, along with banjo players, an Irish balladeer and representatives of ancient Egyptians in their native costumes could all be viewed for the price of admission. The wax figure of Polly was said to mirror that of a withered, hideous old hag. Polly was so distraught over the likeness that after the 1846 acquittal, her first question to counsel was, "Can I sue Barnum now?"[79]

In 1847, a sensationalized pamphlet entitled *The Early and Complete Trial of Mary, alias Polly Bodine* was printed. It painted "a lurid picture of the struggle which took place that night, with imaginary details of the ruthless Polly appearing as an unmerciful hussy who relentlessly clubbed her victims to death while their helpless screams were drowned in the roaring wind."[80] In later years, the melodramatic fiction was widely dismissed, but at the time, a fascinated public devoured the publication. Some believed the pamphlet so outrageous it actually aroused sympathy for Polly.

In later years, it was discovered that Polly's grandfather was the victim of murder. The bloody deed occurred because the killer was intent on stealing the elderly gentleman's money, which he kept at home. The perpetrator was found, convicted and hanged.

On February 5, 1850, Polly Bodine wrote to the *New York Herald* regarding a published article:

> *Sir—Being a daily reader of your entertaining paper, the* Herald, *I see from your Philadelphia correspondent that they…are honored with the presence of one Polly Bodine, and she daily engaged in vending stocks, collars, etc. Now sir, there are many Polly's there, but if it's meant for myself, Mary Bodine of Staten Island, their mistake is great. I have this world's comforts, thank God, without turning pedlar [sic]. Please contradict the Philadelphia correspondence, and you, as a gentleman, will oblige me, Mary Bodine.*

On February 7, 1850, the paper contradicted the story.

Illustrated woodcuts of Polly that appeared numerous times in New York publications during the trials bore little resemblance and were used for other individuals as well. In 1853, the *Western New Yorker* newspaper wrote that one illustration was used to depict Harriet Beecher Stowe in Barnum's *Illustrated News*. Subsequently, the *Brooklyn Daily Eagle* of August 1, 1857, noted that Polly's woodcut had served to illustrate "Madame Restell—the 'veiled murderess,' and Mrs. Cunningham…and we expect to see it…as Miss Madaline Smith."

Owing to George Housman's devotion to his sister at the trials, it was claimed that he remarked that a man can "get a wife anytime, but he couldn't another sister."[81] George died in 1886 at the age of seventy-eight. With George's death, Polly, at seventy-six, was the last living sibling.

On July 28, 1892, undertaker John Steers pulled a hearse and closed carriage to the front of Polly's Lafayette Avenue home. He and his assistant removed a black-velvet, silver-mounted coffin from the house. With bowed heads and a sob, a gray-haired man and woman followed arm in arm behind them. Dressed in mourning, the woman had "a thick veil of crape" across her face, making her unrecognizable. As the coffin was placed inside the funeral wagon, the woman lamented, "Oh mother, it cannot be that you are gone." Albert Bodine attempted to comfort his sister by patting her on the cheek as he gently asked her not to make a scene. The carriage and hearse then took a "circuitous" route to Fairview Cemetery on the Richmond Turnpike at Meier's Corners. "No choir was there, nor even a clergyman."[82]

Three generations of Staten Islanders called Polly Bodine a murderess. Her physician, Dr. Walser, was astonished when a newsman from *The World* contacted him for details about Polly's death, as family and friends had kept quiet on this fact. Stating that her children would be aggrieved to know that the public had discovered her demise, Dr. Walser said that Albert and Eliza Bodine had always believed in her innocence. The slightest mention of Polly on Staten Island brought about renewed interest in her life and the events around her sister in law's demise, a fact that greatly pained her children. They hoped her death would not cause renewed curiosity. Mary "Polly" Bodine died of acute intestinal obstruction at about noon on July 28, 1892. She was eighty-two years old. Several years earlier, she had suffered a stroke that left her paralyzed. Dr. Walser absolutely denied that she confessed to the crime on her deathbed.

Not far from the site of the murder, at Hillside Cemetery in Graniteville, George Housman buried his wife and child. On Emeline's headstone, he inscribed the words "She lived beloved and died lamented." On little Ann Eliza's stone was written:

As like the bright and morning flower,
She lived and vanished in an hour.
Grim Death with wide and ruthless sway,
Made her his mark and seized his prey.

Left: Headstone of Emeline and Ann Eliza Housman at Hillside Cemetery in Graniteville. *Photograph by Patricia Salmon, 2013.*

Below: This headstone was erected in 2005 by the administration of Fairview Cemetery. *Photograph by Patricia M. Salmon, 2013.*

Much has been said and written about Mary "Polly" Bodine over the years. One of the most quoted statements came from the "old-timers of Staten Island," who believed there was "not the slightest doubt of her guilt and that her escape was purchased by her father, who expended $50,000 in bribing jurors, etc. and that he made himself a poor man by the transaction."[83]

Around 2005, the administration of Fairview Cemetery placed a headstone on the unmarked grave of Mary "Polly" Bodine. Unidentified for approximately 113 years, the many individuals who inquire after the accused murderess now have a tangible marker to visit in order to contemplate Staten Island's most intriguing unsolved crime.

NOTES

Introduction

1. Clute, *Annals of Staten Island*.

Chapter 1

2. *Evening Express*, "Another Life at Stake," May 1879.
3. *New York Times*, "The Mystery Still Unsolved," September 27, 1878.
4. Ibid., "The Body in the Barrel," October 8, 1878.
5. Ibid., "Silver Lake Tragedy," May 22, 1879.
6. Ibid.
7. Ibid., "Annie Reinhardt's Death," May 23, 1879.
8. Ibid.
9. Ibid., "Reinhardt to be Hanged," May 24, 1879.
10. *New York Daily Tribune*, "Indignation of a Condemned Man," January 21, 1880.
11. *New York Evening Express*, "Reinhardt," January 14, 1881.
12. *Brooklyn Eagle*, "Expiated," January 14, 1881.

Chapter 2

13. *The World*, "The Doctor Disliked Her," May 15, 1889
14. Ibid., "Mary Tobin's Lover Found," May 16, 1889.
15. *Daily Graphic*, "Bryan's Dead Sweetheart," March 17, 1889.

16. *New York Herald*, "Mary Tobin's Slayer Is Still Unknown," May 9, 1891.
17. *The Press*, "Doctor's Disagree," May 28, 1889.
18. *The World*, "Staten Island's Mystery," May 27, 1889.
19. Ibid., "She's the Woman in Black," July 15, 1889.
20. Ibid., "Very Grave Charges," May 8, 1891.
21. *New York Herald*, "Grave Charges for Dr. Bryan to Answer," May 14, 1891.
22. *The Press*, "As to Mary E. Tobin's Death," May 16, 1891.
23. *New York Times*, "An Enemy Has Done This," September 29, 1891.

Chapter 3

24. *Evening Telegram*, "Premeditated Murder," October 25, 1890.

Chapter 4

25. *The Press*, "It Is the Body of Ruttinger," March 14, 1891.
26. Ibid.; *Evening World*, "On Ruttinger's Body," March 21, 1891.
27. *The World*, "Where's Wright?" March 14, 1891.
28. Ibid., "Ruttinger Verdict," March 31, 1891.

Chapter 5

29. *The World*, "Three Men Kill a Friend," March 19, 1894.

Chapter 6

30. *New York Times*, "Unknown Wakes Doctor and Shoots Him in Bed," January 27, 1907.
31. *New York Press*, January 27, 1907.
32. *New York Times*, "Police Say They Have Dr. Townsend's Slayer," January 29, 1907.
33. *Rome Daily Sentinel*, "Arrest in Townsend Case," January 28, 1907.
34. *New York Times*, "Jury Holds John Bell for Townsend Murder," February 7, 1907.
35. Ibid., "He Killed Dr. Townsend, Bell's Relatives Say." January 31, 1907.
36. Ibid.
37. *New York Daily Tribune*, "Bell Hinted Suicide," January 30, 1907.
38. *New York Times*, "He Killed Dr. Townsend, Bell's Relatives Say," January 31, 1907.
39. Ibid.
40. *The Sun*, "Circumstances Against Bell," January 30, 1907.

41. *Daily Standard Union*, "Two Arrests in Townsend Murder Case," February 3, 1907.

42. *New York Times*, "Bell Told of Murder Witnesses Testify," May 22, 1907.

43. Ibid., "Tombstone Mark in the Bell Case," May 23, 1907

44. Ibid., "Bell Found Guilty," May 24, 1907.

45. Herold, "Father's Death Left Decades of Anguish," *Mercury News*, January 25, 2007.

Chapter 7

46. *New York Tribune*, "Man Killed in Auto Believed 'Bootlegger,'" August 22, 1920.

47. Ibid.

48. *New York Times*, "Dry Agents Killed Eckett, Police Say," August 23, 1920.

49. *Evening World*, "Eckert Killed to Shield 'Whiskey Ring,' Police Say; Find New Clue to Slayer," August 23, 1920.

50. Reycraft, "1920—The First Racketeer," *Staten Island Advance*, September 1, 1951.

51. *New York Times*, "Leading Residents Called in Rum Quiz," September 1, 1920.

52. Ibid., "Politics in Eckert Case, Says Tiernan," August 29, 1920.

53. Ibid., "Tiernan Indicted as a Bootlegger," September 3, 1920.

54. Reycraft, "1920—The First Racketeer," *Staten Island Advance*, September 1, 1951.

Chapter 8

55. *New York Times*, "Official Accused of Bootlegging," March 18, 1921.

56. *Syracuse Herald*, "Wife Fails to Save McNally from Chair," September 9, 1921.

57. *New York Tribune*, "'I Am Innocent,' McNally Insisted on Eve of Execution," September 17, 1921.

Chapter 10

58. *New York Times*, "Youth Confesses He Strangled Girl," November 4, 1928.

59. Ibid.

60. *New York Evening Press*, "Slain Girl Buried; Priest Not on Hand," November 6, 1928.

61. *Standard Union*, "Rice Arraigned for S.I. Murder," November 9, 1928.

62. Ibid., "Vincent Rice Pleads Guilty to Murder," December 17, 1928.

63. *New York Times*, "Rice Pleads Guilty of Killing Girl," December 18, 1928.

64. *Pawling Chronicle*, "Slayer Who Feared Kiss Is Given Life," no date.

Chapter 11

65. *New York Times*, "Brown Hat and Coat Lone, Vague Clue to Mrs. Bauer's Slayer," March 27, 1924.
66. Ibid., "Hoffman Identified; Friend Shatters His Bauer Murder Alibi," April 20, 1924.
67. Ibid.
68. Ibid., "Hoffman to Enter Prison Tomorrow," May 30, 1924.
69. Ibid., "Hoffman in Tears as Mother Calls," May 31, 1924.
70. Ibid., "Hoffman Asks Kings Trial," May 2, 1928; Ibid., "Hoffman on Trial Third Time," November 8, 1928.
71. Ibid., "Hoffman on Stand in His Own Defense," November 24, 1928.
72. Ibid., "Jury Is Locked Up in Murder Case," November 27, 1928.
73. Ibid., "Hoffman Acquitted of Bauer Murder," May 23, 1929.

Chapter 12

74. Clemens, "The Staten Island Mystery of 1843." *The Era Magazine: An Illustrated Monthly*.
75. *New York Herald*, "Further Particulars of the Murder at Staten Island," January 3, 1844.
76. *Morning Courier and New York Enquirer*, "The Staten Island Murder," January 16, 1844.
77. *Brooklyn Daily Eagle*, "Richmond County Oyer and Terminer," June 28, 1844.
78. *Evening Telegraph*, "Some Fool Juries," June 11, 1899.
79. *The Sun*, "Old Times in the Courts," July 5, 1896.
80. Warnshuis, "Graniteville Murder of Christmas Eve 1843," *Staten Island Advance*, December 24, 1943.
81. *The World*, "Polly Bodine's Brother," 1886.
82. Ibid., "Half a Century of Odium," July 29, 1892; *New York Herald*, "Death of Polly Bodine," July 29, 1892.
83. *Oneida Free Press*, "A Murderer's Hopes," 1881.

BIBLIOGRAPHY

Clute, John J. *Annals of Staten Island*. New York: Heart of the Lakes Publishing, 1986.
Leng, Charles W., and William T. Davis. *Staten Island and Its People*. 2 vols. New York: Lewis Historical Publishing Company, 1930.

Chapter 1: The Body in the Barrel

Brooklyn Eagle. "Expiated." January 14, 1881.
Evening Express. "Another Life at Stake." May 1879.
New York Evening Express. "Reinhardt." January 14, 1881.
New York Times. "Annie Reinhardt's Death." May 23, 1879.
———. "The Body in the Barrel." October 8, 1878.
———. "The Mystery Still Unsolved." September 7, 1878.
———. "Reinhardt to be Hanged." May 24, 1879.
———. "Silver Lake Tragedy." May 22, 1879.
New York Tribune. "Indignation of a Condemned Man." January 21, 1880.

Chapter 2: Dead Among the Rocks

New York Herald. "Grave Charges for Dr. Bryan to Answer." May 14, 1891.
———. "Mary Tobin's Slayer Is Still Unknown." May 9, 1891.
New York Times. "An Enemy Has Done This." September 29, 1891.

———. "As Told to the Coroner." May 17, 1889.

Pittsburg Dispatch. "The Fire Record." September 29, 1891.

The Press. "As to Mary Tobin's Death." May 16, 1891.

———. "Doctor's Disagree." May 28, 1889.

The Sun. "Dr. Bryan and Miss Tobin." May 21, 1889.

———. "Staten Island's Mystery." May 15, 1889.

The World. "Deeper Mystery." May 14, 1889.

———. "The Doctor Disliked Her." May 15, 1889.

———. "Mary Tobin's Fate." May 16, 1889.

———. "Mary Tobin's Lover Found." May 16, 1889.

———. "Said to be Mary Tobin." May 13, 1889.

———. "She's the Woman in Black." July 15, 1889.

———. "Staten Island's Mystery." May 27, 1889.

———. "Very Grave Charges." May 8, 1891.

Chapter 3: A Wicked Love

Albany Evening Journal. "Odell Pardons Life Convict." June 12, 1901.

Evening Telegram. "Premeditated Murder." October 25, 1890.

New York Herald. "To Sing Sing for Life." January 16, 1891.

———. "The Story of the Lifers at Sing Sing." November 29, 1903.

New York Times. "General McAlpin Gets Convict Released." June 12, 1901.

The Press. "Murdered by a Jealous Lover." October 25, 1890.

———. "Murdered Mrs. Owens Photographed" October 26, 1890.

The Sun. "Emmons' Wretched Life." October 26, 1890.

———. "Murderer Emmons Pardoned." November 8, 1891.

The World. "Emmons Goes to Sing Sing for Life." January 16, 1891.

———. "Emmons' Love Was Fatal." October 25, 1890

———. "Is Emmons a Sane Man?" January 15, 1891.

Chapter 4: The Great Tottenville Mystery

Evening Express. "Tell-Tale Boot Marks." March 17, 1891.

Evening World. "Is Wright Dead Too?" March 16, 1891.

New York Herald. "Ruttinger's Policy Paid." February 16, 1892.

New York Times. "Fred Evans Identified." March 19, 1891.

———. "Old Straw Rethrashed." March 22, 1891.

———. "Perrin H. Sumner Dies in Subway." March 20, 1914.

The Press. "It Is the Body of Ruttinger." March 14, 1891.

The Sun. "Not a Good Enough Edgar." February 6, 1891.

———. "Sumner Arrested Again." April 1, 1891.

The World. "Ruttinger Verdict." March 31, 1891.

———. "Wright Lies in Greenwood." April 2, 1891.

Chapter 5: The Staten Island Terror

New York Herald. "Assaulted by Three Men." March 19, 1894.

New York Times. "Beaten to Death by Three Men." March 19, 1894.

———. "Harry Keeley, Ex-Convict, Insane." October 17, 1903.

———. "He Hated the Police and Shot a Policeman." June 29, 1903

Poughkeepsie Eagle-News. "May Be Freed After 16 Years in Matteawan." December 20, 1919.

The World. "Three Men Kill a Friend." March 19, 1894.

Chapter 6: Revenge Renews Our Happy Love in Heaven Forever

Daily Standard Union. "Two Arrests in Townsend Murder Case." February 3, 1907.

Herhold, Scott. "Father's Death Left Decades of Anguish." *Mercury News*, January 25, 2007.

New York Press. January 27, 1907.

New York Times. "Bell Found Guilty." May 24, 1907.

———. "Bell Told of Murder Witnesses Testify." May 22, 1907.

———. "Condemned Man Insane." July 17, 1910.

———. "Couldn't Identify Bell." February 6, 1907.

———. "Dr. Emma Townsend Dead." September 14, 1916.

———. "He Killed Dr. Townsend, Bell's Relatives Say." January 31, 1907.

———. "Police Say They Have Dr. Townsend's Slayer." January 29, 1907.

———. "Suspect Arrested Here for Townsend Shooting." January 28, 1907.

———. "Tombstone Mark in the Bell Case." May 23, 1907.

———. "Unknown Wakes Doctor and Shoots Him in Bed." January 27, 1907.

New York Tribune. "Bell Hinted Suicide." January 30, 1907.

———. "Doctor Shot in Bed." January 27, 1907.

Rome Daily Sentinel. "Arrest in Townsend Case" January 28, 1907.

The Sun. "Circumstances Against Bell." January 30, 1907.

Chapter 7: Three Bullets for the Bootlegger

Evening World. "Eckert Killed to Shield 'Whiskey Ring,' Police Say; Find New Clue to Slayer." August 23, 1920.

———. "Suspected 'Dry' Agent Said to be Bootlegger, Slain on Staten Island." August 21, 1920.

———. "Third Man Held on Charge of Murder in Eckert Case; Public Officials Named." August 25, 1920.

———. "U.S. Grand Jury Inquiry Ordered into Liquor Plots Bared by Eckert Murder." August 27, 1920.

New York Times. "Dry Agents Killed Eckett [*sic*], Police Say." August 23, 1920.

———. "Eckert Net Enfolds High Official's Kin." August 25, 1920.

———. "Leading Residents Called in Rum Quiz." September 1, 1920.

———. "Official Accused of Bootlegging." March 18, 1921.

———. "Politics in Eckert Case, Says Tiernan." August 29, 1920.

———. "Tiernan Indicted as a Bootlegger." September 3, 1920.

New York Tribune. "Man Killed in Auto Believed Bootlegger." August 22, 1920.

Reycraft, Jack. "1920—The First Racketeer." *Staten Island Advance*, September 1, 1951.

Chapter 8: Life for the Murderer, Death for Complicity

Brooklyn Standard Union. "McNally Is Executed; Last Hours With Wife." September 16, 1921.

Evening Telegram. "Doomed, Hears Pleas for Life and of Baby's Death." August 28, 1921.

New York Times. "Get $10,000 in Furs After Alarm Rings." December 13, 1920.

———. "Official Accused of Bootlegging." March 18, 1921.

———. "Witness Gives Clue to Woman's Murder." March 17, 1921.

New York Tribune. "'I Am Innocent,' McNally Insisted on Eve of Execution." September 17, 1921.

———. "McNally Dies in Chair for Restaurant Murder." September 16, 1921.

Syracuse Herald. "Wife Fails to Save McNally from Chair." September ? 1921.

Chapter 9: The Baby Farm Murder

New York Times. "Dogs Hunt Suspect in Woman's Murder." July 1, 1927.

———. Woman Shot Dead on Staten Island." June 30, 1927.

Poughkeepsie Eagle-News. "Owner of Baby Farm Is Found Guilty." February 28, 1924.

Reycraft, Jack. "1927—The Oakwood Heights Slaying." *Staten Island Advance*, October 3, 1951.

Sullivan, Gerard. "Who Murdered These 8 Women?" *Staten Island Advance*, January 9, 1932.

Chapter 10: The Kiss Slayer

Brooklyn Daily Eagle. "Boy Sweetheart Admits He Killed Strangled Girl." November 3, 1928.

Daily Argus. "Rice Unperturbed at News of Indictment." November 6, 1928.

New York Evening Post. "Rice, Slayer, Gets 20 Years to Life." December 20, 1928

New York Evening Press. "Slain Girl Buried; Priest Not on Hand." November 6, 1928.

New York Times. "Girl Found Slain in Richmond Home." November 3, 1928.

————. "Rice Pleads Guilty of Killing Girl." December 18, 1928.

————. "Youth Confesses He Strangled Girl." November 4, 1928.

Pawling Chronicle. "Slayer Who Feared Kiss Is Given Life." No date.

Standard Union. "Rice Arraigned for S.I. Murder." November 9, 1928.

————. "Vincent Rice Pleads Guilty to Murder." December 17, 1928.

Chapter 11: The Movie Projectionist Murderer?

New York Times. "Brown Hat and Coat Lone, Vague Clue to Mrs. Bauer's Slayer." March 27, 1924.

————. "Hoffman Asks Kings Trial." May 2, 1928.

————. "Hoffman Identified; Friend Shatters His Bauer Murder Alibi." April 20, 1924.

————. "Hoffman Jury Out; Prisoner Cries 'Lie' Under State's Fire." May 29, 1924.

————. "Hoffman Pleads for Speedy Trial." April 28, 1924.

————. "Hoffman to Enter Prison Tomorrow." May 30, 1924.

Chapter 12: That Most Wicked and Wretched Woman

Brooklyn Daily Eagle. "The News Illustrated." August 1, 1857.

————. "Richmond County Oyer and Terminer." June 28, 1844.

Clemens, Will T. "The Staten Island Mystery of 1843." *The Era Magazine: An Illustrated Monthly* 14 (1904).

Evening Telegraph. "Some Fool Juries." June 11, 1899.

Morning Courier and New York Enquirer. "The Staten Island Murder." January 16, 1844.

New York Daily Tribune. "City Items." November 10, 1845.

New York Herald. "Death of Polly Bodine." July 29, 1892.

———. "Further Particulars of the Murder at Staten Island." January 3, 1844.

———. "Polly Bodine's Trial." November 15, 1845.

———. "The Staten Island Murder—Committal of Waite." January 7, 1844.

———. "The Staten Island Murders." January 8, 1844.

Oneida Free Press. "A Murderer's Hopes." 1881.

The Sun. "Old Times in the Courts." July 5, 1896.

Warnshuis, Lois. "Graniteville Murder of Christmas Eve 1843 Remains Mystery After Lapse of Century." *Staten Island Advance*, December 24, 1943.

The World. "Half a Century of Odium." July 29, 1892.

———. "Polly Bodine's Brother." 1886.

For a complete index to *Murder & Mayhem on Staten Island*, please contact the author at salmonf@aol.com.

ABOUT THE AUTHOR

Patricia M. Salmon retired as curator of history from the Staten Island Museum in 2012. A Staten Island resident for almost fifty years, she was a naturalist/historian at Clay Pit Ponds State Park Preserve in that borough for eight years. Ms. Salmon has authored the books *Realms of History: The Cemeteries of Staten Island* and *The Staten Island Ferry: A History*. A board member of the Tottenville Historical Society, she is an adjunct professor at Wagner College in Staten Island and a guest contributor to the "Memories" column of the *Staten Island Advance*.

Photograph by Barbara Hemedinger, 2013.